D0394293

JBIO
BUR

Fighters Against Censorship

Other books in the History Makers series:

History MAKERS

Fighters Against Censorship

By Kate Burns

LUCENT
BOOKS®

THOMSON
★
GALE

Norwood Public Library
1110 Lucerne Street
Norwood, CO 81423

San Diego • Detroit • New York • San Francisco • Cleveland
New Haven, Conn. • Waterville, Maine • London • Munich

© 2004 by Lucent Books. Lucent Books is an imprint of The Gale Group, Inc.,
a division of Thomson Learning, Inc.

Lucent Books® and Thomson Learning™ are trademarks used herein under license.

For more information, contact
Lucent Books
27500 Drake Rd.
Farmington Hills, MI 48331-3535
Or you can visit our Internet site at http://www.gale.com

ALL RIGHTS RESERVED.
No part of this work covered by the copyright hereon may be reproduced or used in any form or by
any means—graphic, electronic, or mechanical, including photocopying, recording, taping, Web distribution, or information storage retrieval systems—without the written permission of the publisher.

LIBRARY OF CONGRESS CATALOGING-IN-PUBLICATION DATA

Burns, Kate.
    Fighters against censorship / by Kate Burns.
        p. cm. — (History makers)
    Summary: Profiles some of those who dedicated their lives to fighting censorship, includ-
ing James Madison, Theodore Schroeder, Emma Goldman, Tommy Smothers, Larry Flynt,
and Mitchell Kapor.
    Includes bibliographical references and index.
        ISBN 1-59018-340-1

Printed in the United States of America

CONTENTS

The literary form most often referred to as "multiple biography" was perfected in the first century A.D. by Plutarch, a perceptive and talented moralist and historian who hailed from the small town of Chaeronea in central Greece. His most famous work, *Parallel Lives*, consists of a long series of biographies of noteworthy ancient Greek and Roman statesmen and military leaders. Frequently, Plutarch compares a famous Greek to a famous Roman, pointing out similarities in personality and achievements. These expertly constructed and very readable tracts provided later historians and others, including playwrights like Shakespeare, with priceless information about prominent ancient personages and also inspired new generations of writers to tackle the multiple biography genre.

The Lucent History Makers series proudly carries on the venerable tradition handed down from Plutarch. Each volume in the series consists of a set of five to eight biographies of important and influential historical figures who were linked together by a common factor. In *Rulers of Ancient Rome*, for example, all the figures were generals, consuls, or emperors of either the Roman Republic or Empire; while the subjects of *Fighters Against American Slavery*, though they lived in different places and times, all shared the same goal, namely, the eradication of human servitude. Mindful that politicians and military leaders are not (and never have been) the only people who shape the course of history, the editors of the series have also included representatives from a wide range of endeavors, including scientists, artists, writers, philosophers, religious leaders, and sports figures.

Each book is intended to give a range of figures—some well known, others less known; some who made a great impact on history, others who made only a small impact. For instance, by making Columbus's initial voyage possible, Spain's Queen Isabella I, featured in *Women Leaders of Nations*, helped to open up the New World to exploration and exploitation by the European powers. Inarguably, therefore, she made a major contribution to a series of events that had momentous consequences for the entire world. By contrast, Catherine II, the eighteenth-century Russian queen, and Golda Meir, the modern Israeli prime minister, did not play roles of global impact; however, their policies and actions significantly influenced the historical development of both their own countries and their regional neighbors. Regardless of their relative importance in the greater historical scheme, all of the figures chronicled in the History Makers series made contributions to posterity; and their public achievements, as well as what is known about their private lives, are presented and evaluated in light of the most recent scholarship.

In addition, each volume in the series is documented and substantiated by a wide array of primary and secondary source quotations. The primary source quotes enliven the text by presenting eyewitness views of the times and culture in which each history maker lived, while the secondary source quotes, taken from the works of respected modern scholars, offer expert elaboration and/ or critical commentary. Each quote is footnoted, demonstrating to the reader exactly where biographers find their information. The footnotes also provide the reader with the means of conducting additional research. Finally, to further guide and illuminate readers, each volume in the series features photographs, two bibliographies, and a comprehensive index.

The History Makers series provides both students engaged in research and more casual readers with informative, enlightening, and entertaining overviews of individuals from a variety of circumstances, professions, and backgrounds. No doubt all of them, whether loved or hated, benevolent or cruel, constructive or destructive, will remain endlessly fascinating to each new generation seeking to identify the forces that shaped their world.

A Tradition of Fighting Censorship

Censorship is often defined as the suppression of any form of expression considered objectionable. The expression could be any number of things, like a political speech, a painting, a popular song, a joke, or a nude photograph in a magazine. The reasons for censorship vary as widely as those who call for it, but often the impetus to regulate the media, art, or controversial speech originates from governments, politicians, religious organizations, and reform movements. At the root of most censorship attempts is the claim that the expression in question will do some sort of harm—perhaps to children, morality, or national security. Whether to prevent harm or to gain an advantage that increases their power, those in authority exercise censorship when they supervise or control public communication or conduct. Thus, the censor edits or eliminates the offending expression.

When the issue of censorship arises, many people first think of the extreme end of repression that may be present in governments such as harsh dictatorships and domineering monarchies. After all, when the leaders of a society insist on values and policies that are not favored by the people, they often have to silence dissent in order to maintain their power over the discontented citizens. In this sense, the censors may fear that their subjects will rise together to take some or all of the power that has been hoarded by the few. In medieval Europe, for example, monarchs were known to torture subjects who challenged their policies, and they often performed the punishment in public to warn others of the dangers of defiance.

Yet censorship is a central issue in democratic societies as well, and the United States is an interesting case in point. American history often emphasizes struggles for freedom, both before and after the formation of the United States as an independent nation. When the Constitution was written in the summer of 1787, it had been inspired by fair-minded Native American tribal governments as well as by European thinkers who despised overbearing rulers. The new nation came to be called "the land of the free" and the First Amendment of the Constitution guaranteed free expression by protecting freedom of religion, speech, the press, and assembly. However, the First Amendment did not eliminate struggles over censorship. In truth, it inspired endless debate about what free expression means in America.

In a democracy like the United States, the words in important documents like the Bill of Rights are open to interpretation by the citizens of the nation. When a government aspires to be "of the people, for the people, and by the people," it opens the floor to a wide

A recording industry representative displays a parental warning label as she testifies at a 2001 congressional hearing regarding media violence. Many people feel that some censorship is necessary, especially when it comes to protecting children.

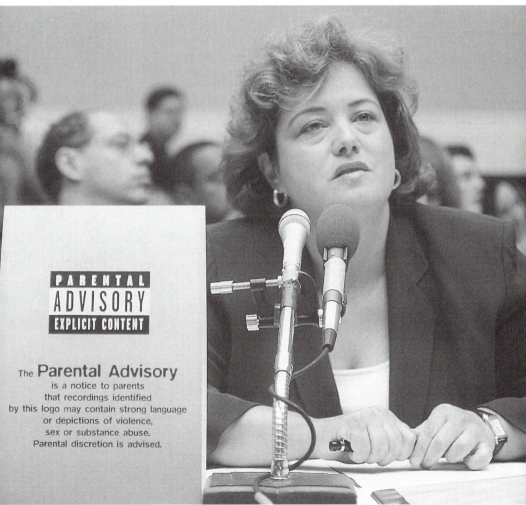

array of opinions. Dissent and debate become essential to a government that is run by the people.

Changes in Free Expression

What constitutes a concept such as freedom of expression is continually under discussion and may change in different historical contexts. On prime-time television in the 1950s and early 1960s, even the hint of sexual relations between a man and woman was considered inappropriate. Some networks required any bedroom scenes involving a married couple to feature two separate beds, and if a man and woman sat on a common bed, they had to plant at least one foot firmly on the floor. Yet in the twenty-first century, displays of romantic affection, whether between married partners or not, abound during prime time. Their frequency and explicitness increase exponentially on late-night network TV or cable channels. Guidelines that define the difference between such things as acceptable sexual imagery and outright obscenity are never finally resolved and put aside; on the contrary, questions recur, inspired by fresh circumstances and innovative technology. When the Internet first offered an exciting new forum for people to share information, some argued that anyone had the right to post whatever they wanted online; others argued that child pornography, hate speech, and government security secrets should be off limits. The debate still rages today. What is the proper balance of freedom and regulation that will allow citizens to achieve individual *and* community goals? What balance encourages people to live together peacefully enough to pursue personal fulfillment *and* mutual safety?

It can be both instructive and inspiring to examine the lives of those who have contributed something important to the American concept of free expression through their struggles against censorship. Despising the censorship he saw in other societies, James Madison wrote the words in the First Amendment to lay a foundation for greater freedom in America. Theodore Schroeder insisted that the First Amendment must be tested and enforced during an era in U.S. history marked by escalating government repression. Taking anticensorship to the streets and the factories, Emma Goldman insisted on freedom of expression for all Americans, including those who held little official power. Tommy Smothers stretched the boundaries of television regulation to open the medium to more

< *A protestor at the 1992 Democratic Convention holds a sign expressing the view that freedom of expression is vital to the political process.*

viewpoints, especially from the perspective of youth culture. Larry Flynt continues to challenge the definitions of "obscenity" used to censor certain sexual and political expressions in America. A pioneer on the electronic frontier, Mitchell Kapor insists that freedom of speech must be protected in the new world of the Internet.

Whether in religion, education, politics, the arts, entertainment, or a mixture of all of these, these fighters against censorship directly influenced interpretations of free expression from the time of the Revolutionary War to the twenty-first century. They responded to technological changes that required questioning censorship related to speech, action, publication, radio or television broadcasts, and electronic communication. They brought their concerns to government offices and courts of law, ghetto streets and union halls, theaters and studios, and computer screens. These fighters against censorship remind the public that freedom of expression must never be taken for granted. Thanks to them and the people they inspired, there is an American tradition of challenging censorship to guard against any dangerous repression that could undermine the liberties Americans cherish.

CHAPTER 1

James Madison: Founder of American Free Speech

Americans who fight against censorship owe a great deal to James Madison. Although he is remembered for being the fourth president of the United States, he is usually praised more for his achievements before he became President Madison. After the American colonies won the war that gave them independence from England in 1783, Madison played a leading role in creating the laws that would guide the government of the new United States. History books call him "the father of the Constitution" because he designed most of the vital document that became the foundation for American democracy. To prevent censorship from happening in the United States, he wrote the First Amendment and led the movement to add the Bill of Rights to the Constitution. Americans who fight censorship depend on the First Amendment to ensure their freedom of religion, freedom of speech, freedom of the press, and freedom of association. Even centuries after his death, Madison's careful words protect people from being silenced or punished for their opinions and beliefs.

Childhood on the Plantation

James Madison was born on March 16, 1751, the first of twelve children to fill the estate of Nelly and James Madison Sr. Since young Madison was given the same name as his father, people took to calling him "Jemmy" as a nickname. Jemmy grew up on the Madison family tobacco plantation, a vast spread of land called Montpelier in Orange County, Virginia. His father ran the farm that had been settled by his great-grandfather in the mid-1600s. Jemmy's mother directed the daily operations of the large household.

As parents, Nelly and James were known to be kind and supportive. Jemmy looked up to his father, but he was very different from him in some ways. James was a strong and healthy man. He loved to work outside and ride his horse around the plantation. Jemmy, on the other hand, was born small and feeble. Extended childhood illnesses kept him in bed much of the time. He preferred to stay inside and read books. His father accepted the differences between them and did not push Jemmy to follow in his footsteps.

With so many brothers and sisters to play with and look after, Jemmy never lacked companionship. The Virginia territory was rapidly filling with other families settling their own farms, and Madison's father kept close relations with most of them since he acted as justice of the peace, vestryman of the local Anglican Church, and commander of the county militia. Such an extensive social circle taught Jemmy the value of fostering family and community support at an early age. The early settlers depended upon such support to surmount natural disasters, defend against retaliation by expelled Native Americans, and cope with illnesses for which cures had not

James Madison authored the First Amendment, which guarantees Americans freedom of religion, freedom of speech, freedom of the press, and freedom of association.

yet been discovered. The fact that only seven of Jemmy's eleven siblings survived to adulthood illustrates the uncertainty of survival in colonial times.

A Young Scholar

In spite of the hardships that all colonists shared, some were better off than others. Young Jemmy enjoyed privileges that many of his neighbors lacked. His father was the wealthiest man in the county. Like many white landowners in early America, James Madison Sr. owned slaves who worked the fields of his plantation. Therefore, Jemmy's father did not have to depend on the help of his son to run the farm. The boy was relatively free to enjoy the books he loved to read and to attend school. When Jemmy was eleven years old, his parents sent him to a boarding school in King and Queen County, Virginia. Since schools were scarce in Virginia at the time, the Madisons were happy to find a scholarly program run by a University of Edinburgh graduate, Donald Robertson.

The rigorous studies inspired the young boy. Jemmy studied logic, philosophy, mathematics, astronomy, and French for several years before he returned to Montpelier to continue learning with a private tutor, the Reverend Thomas Martin. Martin immediately noticed that Jemmy excelled at his studies. He urged Nelly and James to send their bright son to the best college in the area. In 1769 they enrolled young Madison in the College of New Jersey, the distinguished school that later became Princeton University.

At college, Madison gained a reputation as a diligent scholar. More than other schools at the time, the College of New Jersey encouraged its students to develop their independence by learning critical thinking skills. "In the instruction of youth," a local citizen described, "care is taken to cherish a spirit of liberty, and free enquiry; and not only to permit, but even to encourage their right of private judgment."[1] The intellectual environment was perfect for the bookish young man. As historian David Mattern writes, "Madison proved a voracious student, consuming four years of course work in two and graduating in 1771."[2] He received his bachelor's degree in liberal studies and stayed on for another six months to study Hebrew and theology.

Life at college had exposed Madison to a greater diversity of people than he knew on the plantation in Virginia. The experience helped Madison become aware of issues that interested people throughout the colonies. At this time, many colonists talked of war against England. They were tired of being ruled by a distant king who gave them little say in their own government. Some of them had come to the

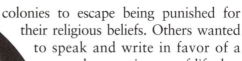

colonies to escape being punished for their religious beliefs. Others wanted to speak and write in favor of a more democratic way of life, but the colonial government censored these ideas, just as British laws had silenced them back in England. A growing number of people prepared for the ultimate form of resistance: a revolution.

Doubt and Despair

Upon returning to Montpelier in 1772, Madison felt a little out of place. The quiet plantation made him restless. He exchanged many letters with William Bradford, a college friend from Philadelphia, and often expressed the frustration of living far from the activity of city life. Furthermore, Madison had trouble deciding on an occupation. Running

Madison's first political cause was the fight for religious freedom in the colonies.

the plantation did not interest him and neither did teaching, the ministry, or law. Historian Jack N. Rakove describes how the young man's refined education had a drawback: "It left him ill-prepared for the life he faced on his return to Montpelier. . . . On the eve of the Revolution, he was a young man possessed of wealth, education, excellent prospects, and no plans." [3]

Madison's ill health left him little energy to pursue a career in any case. During the last months of college he had become very sick once again. The severe nervous disorder only became worse when he returned home. After struggling with persistent illness for most of his life, Madison was convinced that he would die early. The young scholar had many advantages and a promising future, but he saw little reason to push himself if the strength of his body could not keep up with the strength of his mind. This was an exciting time in the colonies as Americans debated whether or not to go to war with England. Yet Madison showed little interest in political issues. When William Bradford wrote to him about the Boston Tea Party in 1774, Madison wrote back, "But away with Politicks! Let me address you as a Student and Philosopher & not as a Patriot now." [4] He would rather read his books than discuss the colonies.

Fighting Religious Intolerance

However, one political issue did eventually capture his attention. In that same year of 1774, Madison became a strong advocate for religious freedom in the colonies. At that time in American history, many of the colonies were controlled by their most powerful church. In Massachusetts, New Hampshire, and Connecticut, for example, citizens had to be certified by Puritan religious leaders before they were allowed to vote and participate in political affairs. In Madison's home colony of Virginia, as in the colonies of North and South Carolina, the Anglican Church of England was in control.

Madison learned that the Anglican authorities had imprisoned a group of Baptists for preaching their religion. The arrest was an attempt to stop the Baptists from expressing their ideas and building the membership of their church. For Madison, the censorship of the Baptists gave him a cause and he found new energy to fight for religious freedom in Virginia. In his opinion, "Religious bondage shackles and debilitates the mind."[5] The college boy, who before shunned politics, was now taking a strong political stand.

Madison began to study other political issues in the colonies. He learned that England had closed the port of Boston and had tightened control of the Massachusetts government to punish the colony for the Boston Tea Party. It was becoming clear to him that Americans could not be free as long as King George III ruled the colonies. Then, Massachusetts declared war on England, and the other colonies followed suit. Madison's fellow Virginians chose him to be a delegate to the Virginia Provincial Convention, a meeting of representatives to decide how to govern Virginia after the royal government collapsed. At age twenty-five, James Madison discovered his calling.

The Act for Establishing Religious Freedom

Over the years that America fought the Revolutionary War, Madison worked in many political positions for Virginia and the united colonies. He served a term in the Virginia House of Delegates, a permanent legislature that was formed after representatives met to form the local government structure at the Provincial Convention. From 1780 to 1783 he represented Virginia at the Continental Congress in Philadelphia. There, with representatives from the other colonies, he worked to create a confederation government to bring the colonies together into a union. After that, he returned to the Virginia House of Delegates for two years to help further develop Virginia's government once the Revolutionary War had been won in 1783. During these first years of his political life he benefited from the guidance of older statesmen. Some of these early mentors, such as Thomas Jefferson and George Washington, became important political allies and life-long friends.

While serving in the Virginia House of Delegates, Madison continued to fight for the cause that was most important to him, religious freedom. The issue surfaced again in 1785 when other delegates tried to secure government support for Anglican churches and their teachers. Both Madison and Thomas Jefferson believed strongly in the separation of church and state in order to protect citizens from religious censorship. Jefferson had written an Act for Establishing Religious Freedom to prevent Virginia from favoring the Anglican Church over other religions. Since he was living in France as a U.S. ambassador at the time, he asked Madison to usher the act through the House of Delegates.

Some of the other delegates were strongly opposed to the act because they wanted the Anglican Church to have enough power to influence political decisions in Virginia. In response to his opponents, Madison wrote "The Memorial and Remonstrance Against Religious Assessments," a document that lists fifteen reasons why state-supported religion is a bad idea. The opening point boldly states that religion "must be left to the conviction and conscience of every man; and it is the right of every man to exercise it as these may dictate. This right is in its nature an unalienable right."[6] Madison's direct and forceful words achieved the desired effect. Citizens throughout Virginia expressed their resistance to state support of religion, and the delegates passed the act into law in 1786.

Proud that he had won the battle for religious freedom in Virginia, Madison wrote to Jefferson that the new law "extinguished for ever the ambitious hope of making laws for the human mind."[7] He felt it ended the danger that those in power could punish people for expressing their beliefs. Many historians have declared this a landmark moment in the process of fighting religious censorship. Rob Boston calls Madison's "Memorial and Remonstrance" essay "one of the greatest documents on religious freedom"[8] in American history.

The Constitution

After his victory in Virginia, Madison turned his attention to national politics again. An issue that concerned him was the limited central government shared among former colonies that were quickly developing their own independent state governments. Without a more powerful national government, he believed, the United States of America would not be united for long. According to Madison and

Thomas Jefferson (left) served as a mentor and friend to the younger Madison, and the two worked together fighting for the separation of church and state.

his allies, a strong central government would encourage the states to look beyond their own interests. There would be less fighting among the states for power and resources and more cooperation to build a nation based on the principles of freedom expressed during the Revolution. In the spring of 1787 Madison spent months studying ideas about building democratic governments. He carefully wrote a plan for a more powerful and secure national government that would still protect the rights and freedoms of individual citizens.

Madison then joined a group of delegates from Virginia to attend the Constitutional Convention of 1787. The convention was called to revise the Articles of Confederation, a document that guided the present loose association of the states. Other groups of delegates from the former colonies gathered in the crowded meeting hall of the Pennsylvania State House.

Guided by Madison, the Virginia delegation took the lead by proposing that the Articles of Confederation be thrown out altogether. They convinced the convention to write a new document, the Constitution of the United States of America. Rather than approach the national government as an association of *states*, the Constitution would define the nation as a united group of individual *citizens* in America, regardless of the states in which they lived. Each citizen would have rights and responsibilities as an American in addition to their state citizenship. By basing the national government on this democratic idea, the United States would be able to withstand any differences or disagreements among the states. Americans would feel loyal to the entire country and work to insure its stability. The delegates agreed to the project.

Madison then presented the ideas he had developed earlier in the year about building such a government. The delegates talked and ar-

At the Constitutional Convention in 1787, Madison was instrumental in convincing the delegates to abandon the Articles of Confederation and draft a new document, the Constitution of the United States of America.

gued and explored Madison's ideas for four months. "Whenever passionate disagreements threatened the enterprise," writes legal scholar Carl T. Bogus, "it was Madison's calm logic to which the others listened. As one delegate put it, it was Madison who had 'the most correct knowledge' about government affairs."[9] The convention finally agreed upon a new Constitution of the United States of America.

Before the Constitution could become law, it had to be ratified by the states. Madison traveled throughout America to campaign for ratification. He listened to the complaints some citizens had about the Constitution. While most agreed with the government structure that was outlined, they felt something important was missing in the document. Many citizens had fought against England because the king had censored their political opinions. Some people had been punished for the ideas they printed in newspapers. Still others had been jailed when they gathered together to talk about the problems in their communities. The citizens of America wanted protection against these and other injustices in a bill of rights that would be added to the Constitution.

Madison promised to lead the movement to develop a bill of rights if the citizens would approve the Constitution. His trustworthy reputation and endless persistence helped the American people understand the importance of making a strong, unified nation. The Constitution was ratified in 1788.

The First Amendment

Although Madison was pleased that the Constitution had been ratified, he knew that more work needed to be done. From the many citizens he visited earlier in the year, he had collected over two hundred ideas for additions to the Constitution. He carefully went through every suggestion and condensed them into twelve amendments describing civil rights and liberties for every American.

He brought the list to the first meeting of the new House of Representatives in 1789 and insisted that the newly elected representatives help him develop a bill of rights as promised. Tired from the hard work of writing the Constitution, many of them resisted the idea of going through the long, exhausting process again. Since the Constitution had been ratified already, some felt they could get away with ignoring the pledge to create amendments. Madison argued fiercely that such a betrayal would undermine the people's loyalty to the new government and finally persuaded the representatives to begin the process of creating the document. After months of debating and revising down to the last word in each amendment, even Madison called the whole thing a "nauseous project"[10] because the arguments seemed endless. Historian Jack N. Rakove states that Madison's dedication to "shepherding the amendments through Congress was a momentous achievement."[11] The final result was a set of ten polished amendments that still stand today as America's Bill of Rights.

In sponsoring the Bill of Rights, Madison took the opportunity to bring his favorite issue of religious freedom to national politics. Yet, his earlier travels and discussions with American citizens had convinced him to expand his notion of free thought to protect all forms of expression, not just religious beliefs and practices. Accordingly, he wrote an amendment that defined freedom of religion, freedom of speech, freedom of the press, freedom to assemble in groups, and freedom to ask the government to address problems in the nation. His creation was the First Amendment: "Congress shall make no law respecting an establishment of religion, or prohibiting the free exercise thereof; or abridging the freedom of speech or of the press; or the right of the people peaceably to assemble and to petition the Government for a redress of grievances."[12] In one simple sentence, this amendment protects the freedoms that Madison had so long tried to uphold.

The Fourth President

James Madison's political career did not end with these remarkable achievements. He continued to serve in the U.S. House of Representatives until 1797. George Washington, during his term as the first president of the United States from 1789–1797, consulted Madison often for advice on how to conduct the new executive government. In 1798 Madison joined with Thomas Jefferson once again to oppose the policies of the second U.S. president, John Adams, toward immigrants and the press. Madison and Jefferson used the First Amendment to argue against Adams's Alien and Sedition Acts that limited free speech in the press and deported immigrants who disagreed with the government. Their arguments rallied widespread American opposition to the acts and helped to elect Jefferson as the third president of the United States. Madison served as Jefferson's secretary of state from 1801 to 1809.

This period also brought love into Madison's life. The lively Dolley Payne Todd caught his attention and the couple married in 1794. Her bright, friendly personality made everyone feel comfortable in her presence. When Thomas Jefferson became president in 1801, Dolley Madison helped him host events since he did not have a wife of his own. She continued the practice when her own husband followed Jefferson to become the fourth president from 1809 to 1817. When visitors came to the White House, the shy president Madison would stay in the background. It was Dolley who ran the social events. As one source describes, "Dolley's social graces made

First Lady Dolley Madison became famous for her charm and social graces while hosting events at the White House.

her famous. . . . Her gracious tact smoothed many a quarrel. Hostile statesmen, difficult envoys from Spain or Tunisia, warrior chiefs from the west, flustered youngsters—she always welcomed everyone."[13]

In his first term as president, Madison spent much of his time negotiating disputes with France, Spain, and Great Britain. Although he settled most of America's problems with France and Spain, the friction between the United States and Great Britain only increased because of a long history of trade conflicts. In 1811 he urged Congress to prepare the U.S. militia for war. The following year, Madison launched the War of 1812 against Britain after being elected for a second term. He sent troops across the Canadian border to hit Britain in its most vulnerable territory, but an untrained and ill-equipped army made little headway. In 1814 British invaders burned the White House and much of the national capital. By the end of that year the Treaty of Ghent was signed to end the war. A relatively quiet period involving reconstruction of the capital and mundane domestic affairs marked the last years of his service as president.

In 1817 James and Dolley Madison retired to Montpelier, his childhood home. Madison turned most of his attention to running the tobacco plantation, but that did not keep him from public life. Always writing, he edited the copious notes he took to record the debates during the Constitutional Convention, and he published many newspaper articles. He directed the University of Virginia for ten years and served as foreign policy adviser for President James Monroe.

Reflecting on his life as an old man, he was especially proud of his work to secure a strong national government that would ensure freedom of religion, speech, and the press in America. In a political testament written when he was eighty-three, the last surviving founding father appealed to Americans to protect their nation in the essay "Advice to My Country": "The advice nearest to my heart and deepest in my convictions is that the Union of the States be cherished and perpetuated. Let the open enemy to it be regarded as a Pandora with her box opened; and the disguised one, as the Serpent creeping with his deadly wiles into Paradise."[14] After turning eighty-five years old, Madison died in 1836.

Madison's Legacy of Freedom

Ever since Madison wrote the First Amendment and it became part of the Constitution, American citizens have had a valuable shield against censorship. In classrooms throughout the country, Madison's words are read to teach young people about their rights. They are quoted in legal cases to protect people from being punished for what they express in speeches, books, music, movies, television shows, stage plays, and even fashion styles. Under the First Amendment, people are free to worship as they please—and they are free to have no religion at all. As one historian says, "the First Amendment to the Constitution has just 45 words, but they are among the most important in the American lexicon. Many scholars believe that the First Amendment was the *first* amendment because it is the groundwork for all our other liberties." [15]

CHAPTER 2

Theodore Schroeder: Testing the First Amendment

Some say it was portentous that Albert Theodore Schroeder was born on September 17, the same date that the U.S. Constitution was adopted seventy-seven years before he came into the world. He dedicated the majority of his life to honoring the Constitution and insuring that its principles guided American legal decisions and political practices. The country, he said, "stupidly went to sleep" [16] after establishing constitutional guarantees for freedom of speech after ratification in 1788. Schroeder took it upon himself to deliver a wake-up call during a time in U.S. history when legislation, law enforcement policies, reform practices, and judicial decisions steadily eroded the right to free expression in America.

First Generation American

Theodore Schroeder was born in a log house in 1864 near the town of Horicon, Wisconsin. When he was five years old, his German immigrant parents moved the family to nearby Watertown where they joined a community of other German families who had settled farms in the area. Before arriving in America, most of the immigrants had participated in the German Revolution of 1848, a war to overthrow the repressive German government and to replace it with a more democratic system. When the revolution failed, they fled to the United States to avoid persecution. They brought with them the ideas about free speech and equality that had inspired the revolution.

The German immigrants became known for their liberal views and their support for the economic improvement of farmers and working people. Although little information about Schroeder's youth has been recorded, he later wrote that the community instilled in him a "predisposition against standardization and an unusual intellectual activity." [17] As a child in Watertown, it seems Schroeder was encouraged to express his individuality, to develop his intellect, and to speak his mind.

Education and Adventure

In the free-thinking environment of the community, young Theodore developed an early sense of independence and adventure. He set off to explore the world outside of Watertown at the age of fifteen. With only fifty dollars in his pocket, he left his parents to fulfill his desire to travel and learn. A job selling women's hosiery and underwear enabled him to support himself for a year. After that, he decided to enroll at the University of Wisconsin, but his course of study was very

Berliners storm the Royal Arsenal during the German Revolution of 1848. Fearing persecution after their revolution failed, many German rebels fled to the United States.

unstructured. He attended classes in the fall and spring terms, and then left to wander across the western United States during the summers.

To fund his summer travels during college, Schroeder found temporary jobs on various railroads. He met a diverse mix of people, including hardworking families struggling to survive, immigrants from many different countries, and hobos riding the rails.

Completing the requirements of a degree mattered little to him; instead, he took whatever classes interested him at the moment. In spite of his erratic approach to education, he encountered ideas that influenced him throughout his life. It was during these college years that he learned to love the words of famous free speech philosophers such as Thomas Paine, Voltaire, John Stuart Mill, and Herbert Spencer. He also admired the writer Robert Ingersoll, who openly challenged religious beliefs. As a child, Schroeder had seen how religious matters had caused his mother a great deal of pain. As a Catholic, his mother had broken family tradition when she married Theodore's father, a Lutheran. Her family promptly disowned her. Religious intolerance angered young Schroeder and he adopted the philosophy of nineteenth-century "freethinkers" who rejected organized religion.

During his travels, he was shocked to discover that Mormons in Utah were being persecuted for their religious beliefs. Reflecting on this discovery later in life, he wrote that the experience made him

The Mormon temple and tabernacle are visible in this 1885 photograph of Salt Lake City, Utah. Intending to defend Mormons against religious intolerance, Theodore Schroeder opened a law office in Salt Lake City in the late nineteenth century.

want to help the Mormons "even as my mother had once had a need for such a defender"[18] against her intolerant relatives. Schroeder had always been taught to value diversity among people and their ideas. His desire to help preserve democratic principles developed into a career path. Eventually, he acquired enough credits to satisfy a major in civil engineering. After he completed his degree in 1886, he enrolled in law school to learn how to fight against censorship and discrimination.

A Lawyer in Mormon Country

Schroeder never forgot the plight of the Mormons and decided to settle in Utah after he finished his law degree at the University of Wisconsin in 1889. He started a law office in Salt Lake City to defend Mormons against religious intolerance. During this period Schroeder courted Mary Parkinson, daughter of a professor of his from the University of Wisconsin. They were married in 1891 and shortly after their daughter Barbara was born.

Unfair legal harassment, political exclusion, and vigilante violence toward Mormons were some of the injustices he battled in court when he first arrived. He also wrote articles against religious bigotry for the local newspapers. The newspapers, controlled by the anti-Mormon majority, eventually declined to print his articles because they called into question their religious intolerance. Schroeder refused to be silenced. With his own money, he printed and distributed pamphlets containing the censored articles.

He also began to realize that the politics in Utah had changed quite a bit since he had visited years before. By this time, Mormon power in the state was on the rise. To his surprise, Schroeder noted that "the Mormons were quite capable of even more bitter persecution of apostates than that which was being inflicted upon them."[19] The young lawyer was dismayed that some Mormon leaders were using their new power to silence their opponents. Schroeder's original interest in the Mormons was due to their status as persecuted underdogs. When he saw how power could corrupt even those who once had experienced discrimination, he changed his strategy and fought against *anyone* who tried to impose censorship in Utah, Mormon or not.

His goal became to keep freedom of speech alive rather than to align himself with any particular group or viewpoint. He took to heart the words of one of his admired free speech role models, the French writer Voltaire, who said "I disapprove of what you say, but I will defend to the death your right to say it."[20] Schroeder wrote in his personal papers, "Most people will defend the claims of right and of liberty for those whose professions and practices are very similar to their own." However, he continued, a true advocate of civil liberties "must defend the claim for equality of right or liberty, even for his most bitter opponents. If he does not do so, a dangerous precedent may be established." [21] The dangerous precedent was censorship.

By 1891, Schroeder was no longer championing only the Mormons. Both Mary and Barbara had died of illnesses in 1896. Schroeder decided it was time for a change and left Utah for the intellectual stimulation of New York.

Troubled Times for Free Speech

As a new resident of New York in 1901, Schroeder immersed himself in the freethinking liberal clubs where he could always find a lively political debate or philosophical discussion taking place. He met many of the leading New York radicals who criticized repressive government policies and economic inequality at the turn of the century. One of these radicals, Moses Harman, had been arrested numerous times for publishing a controversial journal called *Lucifer: The Light-Bearer.*

When Harman was jailed in 1905 for publishing articles about women's sexual equality, Schroeder joined with other lawyers from an emerging organization called the Free Speech League to come to his defense. For Schroeder, Harman was a hero. "Your last imprisonment," he wrote the publisher, "was the means of my giving much thought to the legal status of our 'freedom of the press.' . . . Whatever good may come to the cause of liberty through these efforts of mine, it must in justice be credited to you as one of the fruits of your martyrdom." Schroeder continued: "It speaks eloquently for the breadth of your heroism that you have never suffered imprisonment for anything you yourself had written, but only because of your willingness to give others a hearing. Only those deserve liberty who are willing to defend the liberty of others." [22] Harman's example confirmed for Schroeder that he had chosen the right career. He dedicated himself entirely to preserving freedom of expression in the United States.

The early twentieth century offered Schroeder and other free speech activists plenty of opportunities to fight for that cause. Several decades earlier in the 1870s, a fevered campaign against what some called "dangerous" political ideas and "lewd" materials had emerged in many eastern cities of the United States. At that time, the nation was in the worst economic depression up to that point, and demands for better working conditions sometimes resulted in bread riots or brutal repression of labor strikes. Socialists, anarchists, progressives, and other political groups argued for sweeping changes in the capitalist economic structure to help the poor. At the same time, women were organizing to improve their rights and opportunities. Sexual equality and birth control were seen by many as necessary to the advancement of women. American leaders who did not like these changes were likely to label criticism of the government "blasphemy" and anything sexual "obscene." A young man named Anthony Comstock led this movement with a passion unmatched by anyone else.

Between 1872 and 1874, Comstock and his New York Society for the Suppression of Vice seized over 130,000 pounds of books and 60,300 other items to prevent their distribution to the public.

Moral crusader Anthony Comstock fought for censorship of "obscene" materials. In the 1870s Comstock convinced the U.S. Congress to pass a stringent antiobscenity statute.

*Birth control advocate Margaret Sanger was closely associated with the
Free Speech League, which was run by Schroeder.*

In 1873 he lobbied the U.S. Congress to pass stringent laws against sending or advertising "obscene" materials through the mail. President Ulysses Grant named him a special postal inspector and gave him the power to censor material with official approval. Up until his death in 1915, Comstock used the position to confiscate books and art, to arrest booksellers and public lecturers, to raid art schools employing nude models, and to jail anyone selling birth control. His organization was responsible for arresting more than twelve hundred people in fifteen years. Due to his influence, many states passed their own versions of what were called "Comstock Laws" and started their own societies "for the suppression of vice." Anthony Comstock and others like him helped censorship become well entrenched by the time Theodore Schroeder decided to fight against it in New York.

The Free Speech League

Schroeder's involvement in the Moses Harman case of 1905 brought him into contact with a budding organization called the Free Speech League. At that time, the league was a loose association of a few lawyers interested in preserving freedom of speech. Once Schroeder became the league's secretary in 1905, he almost single-handedly developed it into the leading anticensorship organization in the United States. He led the movement to officially incorporate the Free Speech League in 1911 and it remained active until the formation of the American Civil Liberties Union in 1920.

Schroeder ran the day-to-day operations of the organization. While he administered the league, Gilbert Roe, a law school classmate, defended most of the free speech cases in the court. A famous "muckraking" journalist and league board member named Lincoln Steffens publicized the league's activities. Many well-known radicals and free speech advocates at the time, such as Margaret Sanger, the birth control activist, and Emma Goldman, the famous anarchist, were closely associated with the organization. Largely due to Schroeder's exhaustive research and networking, the league became involved in most every major free speech controversy during its time.

As the league's key administrator, Schroeder emphasized that the purpose of the organization was not to defend any particular viewpoint, but to ensure freedom of speech for all groups and individuals. As historian David M. Rabban states, "When Schroeder believed a case did present a genuine free speech issue, he always tried to help. His voluminous correspondence does not contain a single example of a refusal to assist on ideological grounds." [23] Schroeder made sure that the league maintained financial independence to preserve the organization's objectivity. He refused to accept large donations from individuals or special interest groups because he did not want people to think the league was "the tail of the kite of some other propagandist."[24] He insisted that the league demonstrate "a genuine interest in free speech quite distinct from the person or doctrine of those whom it seeks to help."[25]

A Dedicated Free Speech Scholar

In the years he worked as secretary for the league, Schroeder made it his mission to inform the public about fighting censorship. From 1909 to 1919 he wrote five books about the right to freedom of expression. His first book, *Free Press Anthology* (1909), was a compilation of essays about freedom of speech from writers such as the English poet John Milton, the Dutch philosopher Baruch Spinoza, the French playwright Voltaire, and many others. In his introduction, he explains that he wrote the book because he could find so few materials about censorship at a public library that he visited. He felt a collection of free speech writings was sorely needed by citizens of the United States in order to avoid what he called "intellectual slavery."[26]

His second book, *"Obscene" Literature and Constitutional Law*, was published in 1911. It was the first major work to challenge the "Comstock Laws" and other legislation against supposedly lewd materials. Schroeder was concerned that the laws suppressed all information about sexual matters, including such things as reports by doctors about health issues like venereal diseases. He wanted to insure that each person had a right to seek information about sexuality for his or her mental health. As he wrote in the book:

> Every sane adult person, if he or she desires it, is equally entitled to a judgment of his or her own as to what is the natural law of sex as applied to self, and to that end is personally entitled to all the evidence that any might be willing to submit if permitted. . . . The greatest freedom of discussion is therefore essential as a condition for the improvement of our knowledge of what is nature's moral law of sex, and is indispensable to the preservation of our right to know.[27]

For Schroeder, healthy decisions about sexuality required access to information, and those decisions should be left to each individual rather than to the government.

In 1919 Schroeder wrote *Constitutional Free Speech Defined and Defended: An Unfinished Argument in a Case of Blasphemy*. This book was a thorough examination of the case against Michael X.

Mockus who was arrested for blasphemy, or expressing ideas incompatible with the Christian religion and the Bible. For Schroeder, the decision to punish Mockus meant that:

> Our constitutional guarantee of equality, of freedom of speech, and for a separation of church and state, have accomplished nothing whatever toward the enlargement of intellectual liberty. . . . To confirm judicially the power to punish this man for merely expressing an opinion is to place the destiny of intellectual progress in the hands of legislators, judges and jurors, instead of allowing it to rest in the unhampered intellectual activity of the people at large, where it rightfully belongs in a democracy.[28]

Schroeder argued that censorship by the government took away liberty from all the people of a nation. The victims of censorship were not only the individuals involved in each court case. Once the precedent for censorship is established, it can be used against anyone who falls out of favor with the powerful.

Schroeder also wrote *Free Speech for Radicals* in 1916 and *Free Speech Bibliography* in 1922. Even though he was a practicing lawyer, he decided to avoid the courtroom at this time in his life and focus instead on helping average Americans to understand their legal rights. By making legal information accessible to all citizens, he hoped to pressure judges, lawyers, and legislators to remember that they worked for citizens of the United States, not for any special interest group or to increase their own power. The briefs written for legal cases were "soon lost sight of," he argued. However, publishing information in newspapers and magazines about the cases can "make the court feel that its mental caliber is on trial at the bar of public opinion and that the public has access to all that can be said on the other side."[29]

With this in mind, Schroeder wrote the most significant scholarship up to that point in history about anticensorship and employing the Constitution to defend freedom of expression. He also published magazine articles and composed letters to politicians, legal scholars, and public officials. He freely shared material from his personal library containing the largest known collection of free speech writings and legal cases. Each time he finished writing a publication, he sent multiple copies to libraries across the country and did the same for any important work written by someone else. When he became aware of a local controversy over censorship, he sent literature to selected judges, governors, state legislators, and congressional committees. By 1913 alone, he had sent several thousand pamphlets throughout the United States. During a free speech fight in San Diego involving the Industrial Workers of the World (IWW), he mailed a pamphlet to "all persons whose residence address was given in the San Diego Telephone Directory," [30] as he told a friend in a letter.

Later Years

When the Free Speech League dissolved in 1920, Schroeder had more time to devote to other interests. He developed a theory of psychology which he called "evolutionary psychology" and wrote extensively about applying it to problems in religion, law, criminology, sociology, philosophy, and education. He met and married his second wife, Nancy E. Sankey-Jones, and they moved to Cos Cob, Connecticut, to set up a home.

In 1927 health problems required Schroeder to avoid the cold months on the East Coast, so he spent the winter in the warm, sunny climate of the Virgin Islands. The experience showed him the widespread economic, racial, educational, and political problems of Puerto

After witnessing first-hand the widespread problems in Puerto Rico and the Virgin Islands, Schroeder urged President Franklin D. Roosevelt and First Lady Eleanor Roosevelt to work to improve life for citizens of these American possessions.

Rico and the Virgin Islands at the time. Throughout the 1930s he lobbied President Franklin D. Roosevelt, Eleanor Roosevelt, and other key political figures to improve life for citizens of the American colonies. During the 1940s he worked on collecting and publishing all of the research and writing he had completed over his life.

Fighting to the End

Along with his other interests, Schroeder remained a prolific anti-censorship writer and activist up until his death at age eighty-eight in 1953. He is credited as the first legal scholar to publish meticulous arguments using the First Amendment to dismantle censorship attempts by the government and antivice crusaders of his time. In spite of his valuable contributions, Theodore Schroeder has been largely ignored in historical accounts of free speech struggles in the United States, perhaps because he worked behind the scenes rather than in the spotlight of courtrooms and political campaigns. This has caused several modern scholars who know of his importance to lament his obscurity. His vigilant work against censorship inspired the famous U.S. journalist and author H.L. Mencken to describe Schroeder as "having done more for free expression in America than any other." [31]

CHAPTER 3

Emma Goldman: Anticensorship Freedom Fighter

Emma Goldman believed she was born to fight oppression. She often wrote about her "native rebelliousness against injustice and wrong" [32] in her essays and autobiography. Even as a young child, she seemed to possess an innate independence that inspired her to resist adults who tried to control her behavior or silence her opinions. This tendency, aggravated by the harsh conditions of her early life in czarist Russia, taught young Goldman to despise any authoritative power that leads to censorship.

As she grew into an adult, she turned thought into action by becoming one of the most visible fighters against censorship in American history. Whether arguing in her own speeches and writings or defending the words of others, she made anticensorship one of her primary causes. Her protests against censorship in America and beyond often exacted a heavy price, including harassment, prison, and exile. She was willing to sacrifice so much because she came to believe that freedom of expression is an essential element for human development. In her view, it enhances the growth of every child, ensures wholesome relationships between individuals, and fosters civilized and just communities.

A Difficult Childhood

In Goldman's childhood, the most direct source of oppression was her father, Abraham Goldman. Abraham courted Emma's mother, Taube, after she had been widowed by her first husband and was raising alone her two daughters, Lena and Helena. Abraham and Taube married, starting their own family with Emma, born on June 27, 1869, in the town of Kaunas, Russia (now in Lithuania). Abraham openly expressed his bitter disappointment that his first-born was not a boy. Through no fault of her own, Emma became the target of his resentment. Her father's hostility toward her remained even after two more children, both boys, were born into the family.

Abraham Goldman was a stern patriarch, intent on controlling all those around him with an iron hand. Emma angered him whether she did something wrong or not, and he repeatedly degraded and beat her. One day she received a low mark at school for bad behavior. To punish her, Abraham pounded her head with his fists, smashing the comb that held her unruly hair. Helena, her older half sister, tried to rescue Emma but could not pry her away from his grip. He did not stop until he became exhausted from beating her. During these troubling childhood years, Emma received little comfort from her mother, Taube, who was absorbed in her own depression and emotionally distant toward her children. If anyone performed the role of a loving parent figure in Emma's life, it was Helena.

The oppressive conditions of the Jewish ghettos did not ease life for the young girl. At that time, the government of imperialist Russia ignored the plight of the poor. Those in power often deflected attention from their role in the extreme economic and political disparity by stirring up prejudice against Jewish peasants, making them scapegoats for the country's problems. The Goldman family, both poor and Jewish, had to move often to avoid ethnic violence and to find enough work to survive. Abraham seemed to vent his frustration at such unfair conditions by being cruel to his children, especially to Emma.

In addition to feeling rejected and dominated by her father, young Emma felt stifled in school. Due to the family's frequent moving, her education was constantly interrupted; however, she did attend four years of a Jewish elementary school. The young girl excelled in her studies and loved the beautiful stories she read in literature, but the strict rules of conduct clashed with her free spirit. Her resistance to authority caused some of her teachers to label her a troublemaker. One of her instructors used to beat the palms of her hands when she missed an answer in class. In retaliation, she devised schemes to annoy him such as sticking pins in his chair, tying his coattails to the table legs, or putting snails in his pockets. Remembering this time in her life, Emma later remarked, "[School] is for the child what the prison is for the convict and the barracks for the soldier."[33] She felt that formal education taught children to censor their true feelings and thoughts. Self-education was her preference, and she devoured all the books she could find or borrow whenever she had free time.

Emma's difficulties followed her as she grew into a young woman. Her father considered her constant reading to be in defiance to his authority and against the traditional expectations of young women in Russia. One day he threw her books into the hearth fire and shouted "Girls do not have to learn much!"[34] When Emma turned fifteen, her father took her to a dreary factory job, signing her up to work more than ten hours a day making women's corsets.

Emma hated the grueling labor, but it opened her eyes to the harsh life of the many poor workers in Russia. She began to listen to the hushed voices of labor organizers and political dissidents in the factories and on the streets. Inspired by their vision of prosper-

A policeman whips a Jew in nineteenth-century Russia. Raised in a poor and strict Jewish family, Emma Goldman suffered a harsh and difficult childhood in czarist Russia.

ity and equality for all, she secretly read the forbidden literature of revolutionary Russian and German writers. This taught her about censorship and set the stage for her lifelong campaign to preserve freedom of speech.

She was learning to question all of the expectations and conventions in her society that did not fit her dream of a fulfilling and independent future life. When her father arranged to marry her off at age fifteen to a stranger, she threatened to jump off a bridge rather than submit to his demands. Emma finally escaped her father's grasp by catching a ship to America with her beloved sister Helena. They planned to join their older sister, Lena, who earlier had emigrated to start a family in Rochester, New York.

Seeking Freedom in America

Emma and her sister watched from the deck of the ship as they entered American waters in 1885. Mesmerized by the stories she had heard about the "land of the free," she imagined a paradise founded on the equality and freedom of expression she cherished. As she wrote in her autobiography: "Helena and I stood pressed to each other, enraptured by the sight of the harbour and the Statue of Liberty suddenly emerging from the mist. . . . We, too, Helena and I, would find a place in the generous heart of America. Our spirits were high, our eyes filled with tears."[35]

Although she was poor, only sixteen years old, and spoke little English, Emma was ready to accept the challenge of forging a new life in the United States. However, the young woman's hopes were crushed in only a few months time. She soon found out that her relatives in America had the same ideas about a woman's subservient role that Emma's father did in Russia. Similarly, her Russian immigrant neighbors laughed at her dreams of achieving education and independence. Biographer Alix Kates Shulman describes Goldman's disillusionment: "Like many other immigrants from Eastern Europe, she came seeking freedom and opportunity, only to find instead repression, squalor, and hard times."[36]

Much like in Russia, Goldman's first American job required her to work a ten-and-a-half-hour day and it paid only $2.50 a week—barely enough for her to survive. Once again, she was attracted to the radical thinkers in the factories who discussed how to relieve the economic oppression of the poor. She was shocked to discover that their ideas were censored in the United States, just as they had been in Russia, by factory owners and government officials through workplace harassment, threat of deportation, and police brutality. The "land of the free" seemed to be more of a myth than a reality.

The extreme disappointment Goldman felt, combined with miserable working conditions and her repeated struggles with tuberculosis, led her to seek refuge in a marriage to Jacob Kershner, a Russian immigrant textile worker. After quitting her job in 1887 to take on the traditional role of the wife, she quickly became isolated and unhappy. Increasing tension at home compelled her to seek fulfillment elsewhere. She began to attend the secret meetings of the exciting revolutionary groups fighting against poverty and repression.

A Turning Point

At this time, an incident occurred that changed Goldman's life forever. In the spring of 1886 she read newspaper accounts telling of large crowds rallying against labor conditions in the city of Chicago. On May 4 a group of people gathered in Chicago's Haymarket Square to protest police brutality in the recent labor demonstrations. The protest was peaceful; nevertheless, the police soon arrived to break up the meeting. Suddenly, someone threw a bomb into the dispersing crowd and police began firing their guns indiscriminately. At the end of the chaos, several police officers and civilians were killed and many more were injured.

To add to the tragedy, innocent individuals were blamed for the incident. Without any compelling evidence to connect them to the bombing, the leaders of the demonstration were indicted and eventually sentenced to death. Many saw the conviction as a severe form of censorship and denounced the execution as an attempt to silence those who disagreed with the government and the oppressive working conditions in the factories. For Goldman, it proved how little freedom of speech was respected in America.

On the night of the execution, she wept for the men who were hanged; yet, she also felt inspired and motivated by their example of courage and vigilance. She wrote in her memoirs that "something new and wonderful had been born in my soul" because the incident gave her "a great ideal, a burning faith" [37] in the cause of fighting injustice and censorship. This turning point was so important to Goldman that she considered it the true beginning of her life.

Forging Her Own Way

To honor her new commitment to political life, Goldman wanted to make any changes necessary to live according to her principles and dreams. She rejected all conventions, rules, and even laws with which she did not agree. Risking the stigma of divorce at the time, Goldman left her husband in 1889 and set off alone from Rochester for New York City. From that point on, she refused to marry her

The events surrounding the 1886 Haymarket Square Riot angered Goldman, and inspired her to fight against injustice and censorship.

romantic partners, in spite of having several long-term relationships with men. She believed marriage was an unequal social and legal institution that stifled women and inhibited their participation in community affairs. Although she loved children, she also decided to forego motherhood in order to devote herself to public life.

Since the men she admired who were executed for the Haymarket affair called themselves "anarchists," Goldman set out to explore the anarchist movement in New York. She learned that anarchism was defined as "the philosophy of a new social order based on liberty unrestricted by man-made law; the theory that all forms of government rest on violence and are therefore wrong and harmful, as well as unnecessary." [38] This viewpoint fit into her personal conviction that individuals had the natural right to seek and express their own direction in life. It also confirmed her belief that individuals could build better communities through cooperation and compassion, rather than through the capitalist values of competition and domination. Having found her political home, she quickly became active in local anarchist politics.

Goldman not only insisted on the freedom to live the way she wanted to, she saw the importance of fighting for everyone's freedom of thought and expression. In both her public activism and private relationships, she strived to live according to the ideal of absolute freedom. As she matured into a leader of the anarchist movement, a central focus of her work was to carry the banner of freedom of speech across the United States and Europe.

Goldman fought at home in the anarchist movement, and committed herself to living and fighting for the ideal of absolute freedom.

Learning to Speak Out

At first, Goldman resisted the idea that she could become a public leader in the fight against censorship and other forms of injustice. Few women had visible leadership roles at the time, and she could not yet speak English as fluently as she could Russian and German. It took the encouragement of Johann Most, a famous anarchist orator, to convince her to attempt public speaking. He showed her how to polish her speaking skills by addressing small groups on the street and at political meetings. Then, he organized her first lecture tour of several eastern cities. It was only six months after she had begun her new life in New York and she was terrified; he practically had to force her onto the departing train to start her tour.

At her first large public lecture in Rochester, New York, she froze when she looked at the crowd. The words of her speech vanished from her memory. Trying to compose herself, she remembered the activists who were killed during the Haymarket incident. Recalling their sacrifice for freedom of speech helped her to find confidence. She began her lecture, but she did not deliver the speech Johann Most had prepared for her. She wrote that instead,

> Words I had never heard myself utter before came pouring forth, faster and faster. They came with passionate intensity; they painted images of heroic men on the gallows, their glowing vision of an ideal life, rich with comfort and beauty: men and women radiant in freedom, children transformed by joy and affection. . . . I was conscious only of my own words, of my ecstatic song. [39]

When she finished her speech, the crowd roared with applause. That day in 1889 she discovered she had a gift: to inspire people through public speaking. From then on, Goldman utilized her talent to speak her mind and demand freedom of speech for all people who wanted a voice in the governing of their lives.

Fighting Against Censorship

Goldman often paid dearly for exercising her freedom of speech. When she began her public speaking career in the late nineteenth century, tolerance was low for the topics she chose to address. Government officials, as well as many civic and religious leaders, denounced her open discussion of anarchism and socialism, equality for women and racial minorities, the need for birth control, and free love between men and women unencumbered by expectations of marriage and parenthood. The intolerance often led to censorship.

In 1893 she was arrested for advising a crowd of hungry, unemployed workers to organize street demonstrations to demand food and jobs. She felt that simply voting and petitioning elected officials was not enough to help the desperate families before they starved. The police accused her of inciting a riot and threw her in jail. During her trial, Goldman defended herself by delivering an eloquent appeal for her constitutional right of free speech. She denounced the constant threats she received from police and vigilantes trying to silence her lectures. In spite of her thoughtful reasoning, she lost her case and spent ten months doing hard labor at Blackwell's Island Penitentiary in New York. This prison experience was only one of many sacrifices she made to fight against censorship.

Freedom of speech became even more difficult to defend in the United States as the country experienced the first decades of the twentieth century. Goldman often found rows of police officers waiting to bar her from lecture halls before she could address waiting crowds. It became so difficult for her to lecture without being arrested that in one instance she even chained herself to a podium to prevent the police from removing her before she finished. She was jailed again in 1916 for giving a speech about the benefits of birth control. As soon as she was released, she defiantly went right back out to deliver the same speech again several times.

The continued harassment she received never stopped Goldman from organizing hundreds of lecture tours, free speech events, and fundraisers to defend others who were arrested for their beliefs. In 1911, a typical year for her, she delivered more than 150 lectures in fifty cities; in 1915 she presented 321 lectures. She also became an active supporter of the leading organization to defend First Amendment rights, the Free Speech League.

Mother Earth Magazine

From 1906 to 1917 Goldman also took a central role in fighting for freedom of the press by publishing her own anarchist journal called *Mother Earth*. Goldman and her contributing writers chronicled the rise of industrial unions, women's rights, the birth control movement, free speech struggles, education and prison reform, and poverty and homelessness. Historian Peter Glassgold describes the pioneering magazine as a cultural centerpiece. "During the twelve years of its life," he writes, "the magazine did more than report and comment on the contemporary scene—it was an essential part of the action." [40]

Goldman's unrelenting determination to discuss subjects considered socially taboo or politically unpopular made *Mother Earth* a

Goldman speaks about the need for birth control to a large crowd in New York's Union Square Park in 1916. Goldman became famous for her eloquent and inspirational public lectures.

regular target of government censorship authorities. By that time, Anthony Comstock had been appointed a special agent for the post office to prevent distribution through the U.S. mail of any materials he found to be obscene or politically dangerous. He and his team of inspectors regularly confiscated issues of *Mother Earth* to delay or completely prevent delivery to subscribers.

In response to this kind of official censorship, Goldman said that she found it ironic that Americans stereotyped Russia as an oppressive country but could not recognize the way freedoms were squelched in their own nation. In her essay "What I Believe" she wrote:

> Ours is supposed to be a country ruled by the majority, yet every policeman who is not vested with power by the majority can break up a meeting, drag the lecturer off the platform and club the audience out of the hall in true Russian fashion. The Postmaster General, who is not an elective officer, has the power to suppress publications and confiscate mail. From his decision there is no more appeal than from that of the Russian Czar. Truly, I believe we need a new Declaration of Independence. [41]

The Most Dangerous Woman in America

Although Goldman criticized the U.S. government and denounced some cherished American social customs, she insisted that she felt tremendous love for the country and the citizens of America. She never lost faith in the original intentions of great American freedom fighters like James Madison and Thomas Jefferson. Her concern was that the principles in the Constitution—ideas that inspired thousands of immigrants like her to adopt America as their home—can become lost or corrupted when power is hoarded rather than shared democratically. For Goldman, being a good citizen was more about bravely exposing abuses of power than about withholding criticism of political leaders or pledging blind allegiance to a government. She expressed these sentiments during one of her censorship trials that came after her arrests: "I know many people—I am one of them—who were not born here, and who yet love America with deeper passion and greater intensity than many natives. Our patriotism is that of a man who loves a woman with open eyes. He is enchanted by her beauty, yet he sees her faults." [42] However, her viewpoint was in the minority as the United States was about to enter what would become the First World War.

While America prepared for war, a growing atmosphere of paranoia and patriotism often escalated into strong anti-immigrant sentiment and fear of political minorities. A Russian immigrant and an anarchist, Goldman often received mixed reviews in mainstream newspapers and magazines. Similarly, U.S. attorney general Francis Caffey, who wanted her in prison, nevertheless described her in ambivalent terms when he wrote, "Emma Goldman is a woman of great ability and of personal magnetism, and her persuasive powers make her an exceedingly dangerous woman." [43]

Her position against preparing for war made her even more suspect to many Americans. Then, as the United States finally entered the First World War, the government assaults against free speech

In 1917 Goldman, shown here with fellow anarchist Alexander Berkman, was convicted of espionage for opposing the draft law and sentenced to two years in jail.

culminated in the Espionage and Sedition Acts of 1917 and 1918. These acts made it legal to impose long prison terms on anyone who protested the war. The enemies of Emma Goldman now had a sure-fire way to put her behind bars.

Subsequently Goldman was arrested and put behind bars in 1917. At her trial, Goldman took the opportunity to explain why she believed America's involvement in World War I was hypocritical when it was justified by a call to spread democracy to other countries. "By all means," she said, "let us give democracy to the world. But for the present we are very poor in democracy. Free speech is suppressed. . . . We are woefully poor in democracy at home. How can we be generous in giving democracy to the world?" [44] Once again, she paid dearly for her courageous insistence on freedom of speech. After being declared guilty of "espionage" at her trial and imprisoned for two years, she was stripped of her U.S. citizenship and deported to Russia in 1919.

Living in Exile

At first, Goldman welcomed the chance to return to her original home and join the revolutionaries who recently had overthrown the czarist government. Yet, much like her experience when she immigrated to America, she soon found disappointment in Russia. The new Bolshevik regime there became ruthless in its repression of anarchists and its general disregard for individual freedom of expression. Goldman left the country in two years and published her book *My Disillusionment in Russia* in 1923.

Goldman spent her remaining years moving from country to country in Europe, never feeling a sense of home the way she did in the United States. She occupied herself in part by writing about her remarkable experiences. In 1931 she published her monumental thousand-page autobiography, *Living My Life*. In a famous essay published in *Harper's Magazine* in 1934 she answers the question, "Was My Life Worth Living?"

> Raids on my lectures during my thirty-five years' activity in the United States were a common occurrence, followed by innumerable arrests and three convictions to terms of imprisonment. This was followed by the annulment of my citizenship and my deportation. . . . If I have nonetheless expressed myself, it was in spite of every curtailment and difficulty put in my path and not because of them. . . . Whatever the price . . . [I] feel enriched beyond measure. [45]

Even in old age Goldman remained a vigilant activist. She enlisted in the cause of the Spanish Civil War in 1936, hoping to assist the anarchist revolution there. When the revolution was crushed by Francisco Franco in 1939, she moved to Canada to secure political asylum for refugees of the Spanish war. A free speech gadfly to the last, she worked against censorship in Canada up until her death on May 14, 1940. To honor her final wish, she was buried in Chicago next to the Haymarket anarchists who first inspired her to begin her amazing political life. As the *Emma Goldman Papers* affirms, Emma Goldman was "undoubtedly one of the most notable and influential women in modern American history" whose "role in securing the right to freedom of speech in America is especially significant."[46]

Norwood Public Library
1110 Lucerne Street
Norwood, CO 81423

CHAPTER 4

Tommy Smothers: Comedy Against Censorship

In the late 1960s one of the highest-rated television programs was *The Smothers Brothers Comedy Hour,* a variety show starring the folk-singing comedy team of Tommy and Dickie Smothers. Interestingly enough, the wildly popular *Smothers Brothers* only ran from 1967 until 1969—three short seasons. This was due to the heavy regulation by network censors who aimed to keep TV programming light-hearted and free of controversy. As the *Smothers Brothers* show began to capture the attention of the youth generation, its creative leader, Tommy Smothers, became increasingly interested in the political struggles that rocked the nation at the time. He and his cadre of young staff writers developed the groundbreaking precedent of bringing the concerns of the street into televised entertainment programming. Topics never before addressed so directly, such as civil rights and the Vietnam War, became the heart of what critic Mike Duffy calls their "brash, wickedly irreverent brand of political satire." [47]

Television viewers growing up today might wonder what all the ruckus was about during *The Smothers Brothers Comedy Hour* censorship disputes. The political satire that Tommy Smothers promoted may seem mild compared to the subjects now covered on cable television and even on network comedy shows such as *Saturday Night Live.* However, the conservative 1960s policy of censoring controversial commentary on prime-time entertainment TV had never before been challenged to the degree that Tommy Smothers was willing to do battle. His insistence on pushing the censors' boundaries had lasting effects on television programming. Reporter Marsala Rypka writes, "Tom and Dick made us laugh while challenging us to think about what was happening in the world." [48] Comedy shows like *Saturday Night Live* can present political humor today in large part because of Tommy Smothers's relentless defiance of censorship more than four decades ago.

A Tranquil Childhood

Thomas Bolyn Smothers was born in New York City on February 2, 1937. Over a year later, Richard Smothers was born into the family as well. The two brothers came to be known as Tommy and Dickie. From the beginning, they developed a close relationship that has lasted all of their lives. Tommy tended to be the quiet brother who was introspective and anxious, while Dickie was more outgoing and carefree. "Growing up," Tommy recounted in an interview, "Mom used to say that if she put us in a Cuisinart, she'd probably have one perfect son, but individually we were both very flawed." [49]

Their conventional, middle-class upbringing gave little indication of their future fame. Tommy was named after his father, Thomas

The Smothers Brothers Comedy Hour, *featuring Tommy (left) and Dickie Smothers, often featured political satire that tested the boundaries set by conservative network censors in the 1960s.*

Smothers, who was an army officer. His mother, Ruth, was a home-maker. Military life required mobility for the family, and Tommy moved several times throughout his childhood in the United States and the Philippines. In 1941, after his father died while being detained as a prisoner of war in World War II, Tommy's mother took her sons to Southern California where her parents resided. The boys lived their teenage years near their grandparents and graduated from high school in Redondo Beach, California.

Tommy attended college at San Jose State University and his brother Dickie soon followed him. Sports preoccupied the brothers in college. Tommy became a gymnast and Dickie spent his extracurricular time running on the track team.

The Smothers Brothers, with their unique mix of folk music and satirical humor, developed a large following among young people in the early 1960s.

Budding Comedian

In addition to his interest in sports, Tommy learned to play the guitar and sing the folk music that was becoming popular in the late 1950s. Dickie, too, developed his talent in music and learned to play the upright bass. The two were briefly in a band called The Casual Quintet in 1958, but mostly they enjoyed developing humorous performance duets together that consisted of a mixture of music and jokes.

Eventually, they polished a folk-singing comedy act enough to perform onstage at local clubs. They developed a unique style of satirical humor combined with folk music and used their sibling relationship as the center of their jokes. However, unlike their off-stage personalities, Dickie played the typical serious and practical "straight man" role, and Tommy acted like the silly little brother. It became their trademark that Tommy would jealously complain, "Mom always liked you best!" while Dickie rolled his eyes with frustration.

Their first professional performance premiered in 1959 at the Purple Onion, a trendy club in San Francisco. By the early 1960s they had developed a large following of younger fans who appreciated their goofy and yet pungent humor that made fun of American life. In 1961 they produced their first record album called *The Songs and Comedy of the Smothers Brothers at the Purple Onion* and it sold well. A succession of comedy record albums spread their fame, and they were invited to appear on the Jack Paar television variety show before a national audience in 1961.

In Tune with the Youth Movement

In 1967 the CBS network was desperately looking for a new show to air during the Sunday 9:00 P.M. spot, an hour of prime-time TV that had been dominated by the ever popular NBC western *Bonanza* for years. CBS wanted a variety show that would lure youthful viewers away from *Bonanza*. Although the Smothers Brothers had little television experience at the time, CBS was willing to take a risk and hire them because of their success with young fans.

No one expected the show to succeed. Many other shows had attempted to rival *Bonanza* on Sunday night, but all had failed miserably. Tommy felt that they had nothing to lose since they were fairly new in the TV business, so he decided to ask for more creative control than was usual. He wanted to hire his own writers and make the comedy material socially relevant to young viewers. Expecting the show to bomb, CBS granted his request.

The first season in 1967 delivered a show that seemed to please a wide variety of viewers. Tommy told a *Time* magazine reporter, "We're so college-looking and clean-cut . . . the [conservative] American Legion likes us and so does the left wing." [50] While the brothers did try to tap into youth culture, their early sketches also attempted not to offend older viewers. Many of their guests were those who appealed to the older generation, comedians and artists such as Jim Nabors, Jack Benny, George Burns, Eddie Albert and Eva Gabor, Bette Davis, and Jimmy Durante.

Eventually, the show began to exhibit less tentative support for the youth counterculture. As Ken Kragen, the former manager of the Smothers brothers, said in an interview, "Nobody expected Tom and Dick, when they went on the air, to be controversial. . . . Their roots were in the traditional comedy. . . . It just happened that their consciousness had evolved beyond that and eventually that became part of the show." [51]

Tommy especially was becoming interested in the questions that many young people were discussing around the country: Is the Vietnam War necessary? Does our country put too much money toward building military strength at the expense of improving education and poverty? Why are African Americans and other minorities treated like second-class citizens? Do women really have equal rights? What will happen to the natural environment if we continue to exploit it? As former manager Kragen says, "It was Tommy that was the creative force, Tommy that was trying to find ways to be provocative and be different." [52]

Once the material on the show started to reflect the concerns of the youth movement, the CBS network tried to prevent the Smothers brothers from presenting such controversial topics by editing or cutting some of their sketches. A friend of Tommy's at the time, Michael Kilian, tells his memories of this transitional period: "What was startling was how relentlessly political the 'Smothers Brothers Comedy Hour' quickly became. What stunned even more was how relentlessly censorial the network became in suppressing their material." [53] Tommy resented the heavy hand of CBS censorship. He and his head writer, Mason Williams, decided to challenge the censorship rather than submit to it. Tommy and Williams agreed that their politically based satirical comedy was the style that was getting the laughs from young viewers.

Early Encounters with Censorship

Interestingly enough, the first material that CBS censored on the show was a sketch about censorship. In this scene, Tommy and another regular cast member, Elaine May, portrayed television censors

Tommy, pictured here performing with comedian Lily Tomlin in 1975, deeply resented CBS's efforts to censor sketches that dealt with topics relevant to the youth movement.

who were making decisions about editing a program. CBS cut the entire sketch. Clearly, the network did not want the viewers to think about how television content was regulated by network censorship.

When Tommy and his writers started creating sketches that implicitly criticized U.S. president Lyndon B. Johnson's war policy in Vietnam, the network stepped up its regulation of the show even more. The main reason for this, according to journalist David Halberstam, was that the president of CBS, Frank Stanton, had close associations with President Johnson. In his position, Stanton was supposed to represent the interests of broadcasting, but "he was also Lyndon Johnson's man at CBS," says Halberstam, and "Johnson would leverage him all the time." [54] Mike Dann, former vice president of programming at CBS New York remembers how Stanton would go to the White House to watch *The Smothers Brothers Comedy Hour* with the president. "It was not uncommon for me to get a telephone call that Sunday night, or the following Monday morning, asking me questions about who is watching over the show and what they were doing and was it in good taste," [55] says Dann.

Tommy refused to be intimidated by the connection between his boss and President Johnson. As Perry Lafferty, former vice president of programming at CBS Hollywood, reports, Tommy "never would let up. . . . Every script was some sort of a battle, and Tommy enjoyed that very, very much. I mean, he liked the truth, and he liked to be met head on because he wanted to do a good show." [56] In response to Tommy's resistance, CBS demanded to see the tapes of each show well before air time. The network's program practices division, made up of professional television censors, would make final decisions about what material to keep and what to cut for each and every episode.

The Pete Seeger Controversy

One of the battles that received a great deal of media attention was fought over the guest appearance of folksinger Pete Seeger during

Folksinger Pete Seeger appeared as a guest on The Smothers Brothers Comedy Hour. *When Seeger's performance of a song with controversial lyrics was cut from the show, a public uproar ensued.*

the second season. Seeger had been blacklisted by the House Un-American Activities Committee (HUAC) in the 1950s for refusing to provide information on alleged Communist infiltration in the United States. For over ten years, the blacklist had been honored by television executives who banned him from TV in spite of his popularity as a musician. Since Seeger was centrally involved in the folk music revival led by millions of young people across the country, Tommy wanted to invite him to sing on *The Smothers Brothers Comedy Hour.*

Tommy convinced the CBS executives that it was time to defy the blacklist and allow Seeger on television. The network agreed, but when Tommy sent tapes of the episode to CBS's program practices division, they objected to Seeger's rendition of a song titled "Waist Deep in the Big Muddy." A ballad about a World War II military officer who dies while insisting that his men cross a deadly raging river, the song laments the stupidity of continuing a course of action that leads to needless waste. The censors had no problem with that part of the song. However, they objected to the last stanza which suggested a comparison between the inept World War II officer and President Johnson. Program practices cut the song from the show because they felt the lines implied that the president was a fool.

The censorship backfired on CBS, largely because Tommy loudly protested to any magazine or newspaper who would listen to him. Historian Aniko Bodroghkozy writes that "The move caused a public uproar. Popular-press accounts were generally sympathetic to the Smothers and Seeger and critical of the network's actions." [57] Thousands of viewers sent letters of protest to CBS offices. The pressure from viewers finally caused CBS to retract its position and allow Seeger to sing the song on a later show. After losing this struggle, the network began to allow more politically charged material into CBS programs. Explaining the change of policy, W.H. Tankersley of the program practices division wrote, "I believe it is safe to say that the Smothers Brothers program is a testing ground from which some refinements of policy are bound to emerge." [58] The persistence of Tommy Smothers helped to open the airwaves to a greater diversity of viewpoints.

Ongoing Struggles with TV Censors

In many ways, the censorship battles between the youthful Tommy Smothers and the older generation of television executives were a microcosm of the generational conflicts raging throughout the country by 1968. The antiwar movement, civil rights movement, and countercultural rejection of conventional American life were all in full swing and largely led by young people. Many older Americans tended to resist radical changes in cultural traditions and social conventions they had grown up to cherish. The ensuing clashes were becoming more and more severe. The charged atmosphere inspired Tommy and his writers to challenge the network establishment more directly.

Tommy decided to bring attention to the network's heavy regulation of his show by creating more comedy routines around the topic of television censorship. In one third-season sketch, three censors in conventional business suits stand in a line beside Tommy and Dickie. The first man turns the pages of a manuscript he is holding. He begins to laugh at the pages he is reading and then abruptly rips the pages out of the manuscript. He hands the truncated script to the next censor, who likewise reads, begins to laugh, and rips out the pages responsible for his laughter. When the third man receives the manuscript, only one page remains. He reads the page and turns to hand it to Tommy, saying, "There's nothing funny in this. Here you are boys, we're through censoring your show." [59] The implication, of course, is that the censors pointlessly remove all the funny material in the show.

As the power struggle between Tommy and CBS executives escalated, some of the show's staff members worried that it was interfering with Tommy's ability to produce a high-quality comedy show. He began to replace humorous sketches with serious moments when he would talk directly to viewers about the censorship battles. In one episode, he had a cast member face the camera and snip a pair of scissors close to the lens while he recited:

> We've done good things on this show, we have done some great things, but you haven't seen them because of . . . the censor. The censor sits somewhere between the scenes to be seen and the television sets, with his scissor purpose-poised, watching the human stuff that will sizzle through the magic wires, and light up like welding shops the ho-hum rooms of America, and with a kindergarten arts-and-crafts concept of moral responsibility, snips out the rough talk, the unpopular opinion, or anything with teeth, and renders a pattern of ideas full of holes—a doily for your mind. [60]

Tommy continued to publicize his confrontations with CBS over politically charged material. He called reporters when CBS insisted on censoring a song performed by Harry Belafonte that criticized the carnival-like atmosphere of the 1968 Democratic convention

Joan Baez performs with the Smothers brothers. When the network censored Baez's song dedication to her draft-dodging husband, Tommy went public with his anger.

and the police crackdown on protesters in the streets outside. Likewise, he went public when the network also censored part of Joan Baez's dedication of a song to her husband who was going to be imprisoned for refusing to register for the Vietnam War draft. Reflecting on his protests during those incidents, Tommy said in an interview, "I'm very volatile . . . I can be a screamer." [61]

On March 22, 1969, Tommy invited his most controversial guest comedian, David Steinberg, to tape a sketch that he wanted to air on the April 6 show. When program practices got wind of the performance, they told him the sketch had to be cut, but Tommy ignored the mandate and held the tape past a review deadline. The network executives leaped at the chance to claim the Smothers brothers had broken their contract. They canceled the show and fired the comedy team.

A Legal Triumph

Once again, Tommy refused to accept this ultimate form of censorship, and he and Dickie filed suit against CBS. It took about four years for the case to go to trial. Tommy's legal advisers told him that it would be very difficult to win based on freedom of speech arguments because CBS was a private corporation rather than a governmental body. The best way to triumph over the network was to charge "breach of contract." This disappointed Tommy, but he understood that the trial was a testing ground for future television shows. If CBS won the trial, it would be very difficult for other TV programs to fight against censorship.

The trial strategy proved to be a smart one. The court awarded the brothers $766,300 from CBS to amend for the breach of contract. Tommy Smothers had won. His efforts were rewarded further when the show was given an Emmy Award for "Best-Written Comedy Variety Show on Television" even though the *Comedy Hour* had been canceled. The Smothers brothers were also awarded a star on the famous Hollywood Walk of Fame. Later reflecting on the legal fight, Tommy said, "You can't tell a comedian . . . 'don't say that word, don't say this thing, don't do that piece,' a comedian is contrary by nature. The more they said 'don't do it' the more it seemed it must be important." [62]

Lasting Effects on Television Censorship

In the years that followed the cancellation of the show, Tommy continued to perform with his brother on stage, on television, and in film. There were attempts to revive their TV variety show in the 1970s and 1980s, but neither try attracted enough viewers to keep it going for long. They hosted occasional television specials, appeared as guests on numerous talk shows and comedy sitcoms, had parts in a few movies, and produced a total of twelve comedy albums over the last four decades. Their most successful venture is their live stage performance that they continue to perform today in many cities in the United States.

Tommy also became a professional golfer and competes in tournaments when he has a break from performing. He also owns and manages a vineyard called Remick Ridge in Sonoma County, California, that produces about five hundred cases of Cabernet Sauvignon wine for commercial sale a year. Tommy says, "Making wine is so close to show business. Wine like comedy, is subjective. Either people like your wine—or your songs, or your comedy—or they don't. Each is a creative process and you're only as good as your last effort." [63] Also, as part of his more recent comedy routines, Tommy has developed a mastery of yo-yo tricks. For part of every Smothers Brothers comedy show, he appears in suspenders to demonstrate his talent with a yo-yo in each hand. He produces instructional videos, Tommy Smothers yo-yos, T-shirts, and other memorabilia as the "Yo-Yo Man." In addition to these business ventures, he spends time with his wife Marcy and three children, Tom Jr., Bo, and Riley.

Since mastering the yo-yo, Tommy has incorporated yo-yo tricks into his routines and makes appearances as the "Yo-Yo Man." Here, Tommy (left) appears at a book signing in 1999 for The Book of Yo *with his brother and the book's author, Neil Feser.*

Although his comedy routines are not as overtly political as they were in the 1960s, it seems unlikely that Tommy Smothers will ever stop fighting against censorship. It was his uncompromising defense of freedom of speech that inspired San Jose State University to bestow an honorary doctorate degree on Tommy, as well as Dickie. The Museum of Broadcasting in New York also produced a retrospective exhibit and seminar on *The Smothers Brothers Comedy Hour* to honor the legacy of the show. Today Tommy's censorship battles during the 1967–1969 TV seasons are studied in university classes covering the revolutionary historical changes during the 1960s. A recent interview revealed that Tommy has kept his passionate position on freedom of speech on television. When asked what issues make him angry in the current context of the new millennium, he said:

> I'm angry at how the First Amendment is being abused. . . . Now, during the strangest time in the history of the world, we consume ourselves with trivia in the news. We have the illusion of freedom of speech, but nobody is saying anything important. . . . There's a litany of things we need to speak out about like foreign policy and what's happening to the environment.[64]

CHAPTER 5

Larry Flynt: "I Absolutely Refuse to Compromise"

Larry Claxton Flynt has single-handedly brought to the American public some of the most difficult questions about the freedom of speech. He built the pornography empire of his *Hustler* magazine on the idea that millions of readers crave a sexually graphic, crudely humorous, and purposely offensive publication. While newsstand patrons lay down their dollars to buy Flynt's porn, scores of other citizens vehemently criticize the pages of *Hustler* as obscene filth. By insisting on an absolute interpretation of the First Amendment in numerous court cases, Flynt has tested the depth of freedom of speech protections in the United States during the last decades of the twentieth century. In his own words, he characterizes the dilemma for many Americans: "The question is, am I a smut peddler or a First Amendment crusader? . . . The debate is never going to go away." [65]

Early Challenges

In Lakeville, a small town in eastern Kentucky, Edith and Claxton Flynt celebrated the birth of their first son, Larry, on November 1, 1942. Claxton Flynt had little time to bond with his new son because he was soon drafted into the army and sent abroad to fight in World War II. When he finally returned three years later, he had a difficult time adjusting to the isolation of the Appalachian hills and fell into a downward spiral of alcoholism and unemployment.

Young Larry witnessed the growing tension between his parents over the years that his younger siblings, Judy and Jimmy, were born into the family. Tragedy hit the Flynts when Judy died of leukemia in 1951. "She slipped away one day while I stood by, helpless and sad," says Flynt. "I did not realize at the time that Judy's death was to be the first in a series of losses for me." [66]

By the time Larry was eleven years old, his parents had separated. His mother took him with her to Hamlet, Indiana, to start a new life. Jimmy was sent to live with his grandmother. When the two boys said good-bye, they did not know that it would be the last time they would

Publisher Larry Flynt has continued to test the limits of First Amendment protection since the early 1970s, when his pornographic magazine, Hustler, *first debuted.*

see each other for many years. Flynt's loneliness in the unfamiliar environment and dislike of his new stepfather caused him to retreat from other children. He remembers his unusual attitude in elementary school: "I began to fantasize about the future and started to dream big dreams. . . . Instead of joining other kids in play, I became serious-minded, living out the dreams in my head. I either worked to earn money or sought the solace of my own company, keeping busy delivering newspapers and performing odd jobs." [67]

Such a single-minded focus on moving up in the world would stay with him for the rest of his life. Hoping to break out of his family's cycle of poverty, he dropped out of school after the eighth grade and devised a false birth certificate so he could sign up for the army. When he started boot camp in 1958, his army file recorded his age as seventeen; in truth, he was only fifteen. From an early age, Flynt did not let legal restrictions get in the way of his plans.

Finding His Way

Flynt enjoyed military life; however, he had to leave when peacetime cutbacks forced the army to reduce the number of enlisted men on the government payroll. Due to his limited education, Flynt was in the first group to go. Disheartened, he tried several factory jobs but despised the low-paying menial work. An entrepreneur at heart, he came up with a plan to be his own boss and make lots of money. He moved back to his childhood home and became a bootlegger. Some counties in Kentucky outlawed the sale of liquor, while others allowed it. Flynt devised a plan to buy liquor in the "wet" counties and drive across the border to sell it in "dry" counties. His business yielded a good profit. Nevertheless, his luck would come to an end when he had to leave Kentucky to avoid getting arrested for transporting liquor.

Flynt tried his hand at a military career again, this time enlisting in the navy. Tired of feeling inferior because of his limited education, he took numerous correspondence classes and advanced up the ranks quickly. He became a radar technician and his high test scores got him assigned to a prestigious nuclear-powered aircraft carrier. At an age when most boys attended high school, he was responsible for supervising and training men much older than he was. He excelled at his job and eventually completed the General Educational Development test that was equivalent to graduating from high school. Most of his free time was consumed with reading, and his favorite books were about business ventures and making big money. Flynt says of this period in his life, "It's hard to explain, but it was a watershed experience for me. The navy and the GED gave me the self-esteem I had always sought. The bonds of ignorance and poverty seemed broken. The whole world was opening up to me."[68]

His personal life soon sabotaged his success. He entered two short-lived and ill-fated marriages. To escape from marital conflict, he drank heavily and regularly used illegal drugs. He left the navy, got into trouble with the law for drunk driving and attempted assault, and served a sentence in the Dayton, Ohio, state psychiatric hospital in order to avoid a prison sentence.

Yet, in spite of so much turmoil, he celebrated the birth of his first daughter, Tonya, and kept his focus on finding a way to prosper on his own. In 1965, at age twenty-two, he finally found a business that he felt he could develop into a lucrative establishment.

Becoming a Millionaire

In Dayton, Ohio, Flynt bought a bar that was failing financially. He fixed it up to appeal to the working-class crowd that he knew intimately. Soon the bar was doing so well that he could buy a second bar, and then a third. The skyrocketing profits enabled him to add on a vending machine business. Then a new trend happening on the West Coast caught his eye; women in bikinis were being hired to dance for the customers in nightclubs. Flynt decided to open his own "go-go" club in Dayton. He called it the Hustler Club and it was an instant financial success. Soon he opened a whole string of Hustler Clubs across Ohio from 1968 to 1971. In 1971 he also started what would become a long-term relationship with Althea Leasure, a young dancer in his clubs. She quickly became his business partner as well as his soul mate. Reporter Allana Nash characterized their relationship as "one of the most unconventional and tender love stories in tabloid history." [69]

Although his vending machine business went under due to intense competition from other companies, his go-go clubs more than made up for the loss. Meanwhile, to encourage loyalty from regular customers, he decided to produce a newsletter called *Bachelor's Beat* featuring stories about the go-go dancers. His customers loved it so much that he decided to distribute it on the street alongside mainstream newspapers and magazines. The idea led to his first experience with censorship. When he applied for a distributing license, several local politicians objected. He writes, "The political establishment in Dayton was ultraconservative and considered the *Beat* a plague on the city. . . . I finally got my permit, but only after much wrangling. Someone finally remembered that the First Amendment applied to me, too." [70] The venture did not make him much money, but it gave him experience in publishing and in fighting against those who wanted to censor him.

He decided to revamp the newsletter to include higher-quality photographs of the go-go dancers and articles about sex. The new *Hustler* publication started as a four-page, black-and-white newsletter. Within a year Flynt expanded it to a thirty-two page, multicolor small magazine. Eventually, the magazine did so well that he decided to sell off his bars and nightclubs to focus exclusively on publishing *Hustler*. He still struggled with distributors who wanted to regulate or censor the publication. Eventually the strong sales convinced many distributors to carry the magazine.

Flynt's financial success went from good to extraordinary when he decided to take a risk and publish some highly controversial photographs. In 1975 an Italian photographer called Flynt about selling him sensational photos of Jacqueline Kennedy Onassis swimming naked while on vacation with her husband in Italy. Flynt knew that publishing compromising photos of the former wife of President John F. Kennedy could meet with tremendous popularity, but it also could bring harsh criticism. He took the chance, bought the photographs for eighteen thousand dollars, and printed four of them in the next issue of *Hustler*. The risk paid off more than he imagined; the issue sold like wildfire on the streets and he became a millionaire overnight.

Flynt met Althea Leasure in 1971 when she was a dancer in one of his clubs. The pair later married and remained together until her death in 1987.

Free Enterprise and Free Expression

However, the increased publicity also brought him more problems. The Greater Dayton Association of Southern Baptists began to organize protests against the local printing company for *Hustler*, pressuring the owners to stop producing the pornographic magazine.

Flynt's Hustler *magazine went beyond what other pornographic magazines had done before by pushing the boundaries of sexual explicitness and by including irreverent social and political cartoons and commentary.*

Flynt was not sure he would be able to print the next issue. In the end, since *Hustler* was the most lucrative job for the printing company, the owners decided to keep printing the magazine. Flynt had won another battle with censorship.

Most magazines at the time relied on advertising to make a profit—few magazines make enough money to survive from subscriptions and newsstand sales. Due to the controversial content of *Hustler,* Flynt knew that keeping advertisements would be difficult since many businesses did not want to be associated with pornography. He devised a strategy to avoid being indirectly censored by advertisers who could manipulate his decisions if he were dependent upon their money. To ensure a financial cushion in case advertisers withdrew their support, he sold the magazine for a higher price. Entrepreneurial success in a capitalist society, Flynt believed, came from satisfying the desires of a specific customer base and gaining their loyalty. If his readers wanted his brand of pornography, he reasoned, they would be willing to pay more to get what they wanted.

This strategy seemed to work; he kept the magazine profitable enough through sales to allow him more editorial freedom. He wanted to keep pushing the boundaries of pornographic publishing by including a higher level of sexual explicitness along with irreverent political cartoons and stories about political and religious corruption. Flynt felt strongly about catering to the preferences of readers that he felt he knew best: the men who came from working-class backgrounds much like his own. Other magazines such as *Playboy* and *Penthouse* rarely targeted this market segment directly. He believed that men like him wanted graphic sex and ribald humor when they purchased pornography. They also enjoyed seeing powerful political and religious leaders made accountable for their actions in his commentary. In this way, Flynt saw *Hustler* as a political enterprise as well as a business.

The Beginning of Legal Battles

As the sales of *Hustler* continued to skyrocket, Flynt found that more politicians and community groups made him a target for censorship. He began to realize that he may have to spend as much time in court defending his business as he did in the office to run it. Prosecutors in counties all over Ohio challenged the sale and distribution of *Hustler,* charging that the magazine was obscene. Flynt believed he was singled out because of the political and social content of *Hustler.* Unlike other pornographic publications, *Hustler* regularly lambasted politicians and religious figures. He considered it his mission to skewer community leaders that he believed tried to regulate sexuality to gain power over ordinary people.

Two people who despised his philosophy were Charles H. Keating and Simon Leis Jr., who brought the first major legal case against Flynt in Cincinnati. Keating founded and funded one of the most aggressive antipornography organizations in the country called Citizens for Decency Through Law (CDL). He assisted Cincinnati attorney general Leis to bring charges of pandering, obscenity, and organized crime against Flynt and several staff members of *Hustler,* including Flynt's girlfriend and business partner, Althea Leasure.

Both Keating and Leis were conservative Catholics who believed the distribution of *Hustler* in Cincinnati tainted the city with smut. They argued that *Hustler*'s hard-core pornography offended the average reader in Ohio and therefore went against the community standard of decency. Flynt felt the charges were ridiculous, but he knew that if they were convicted they could go to prison for up to twenty-five years. He took the charges seriously and worked to build a convincing defense for the trial.

In addition to hiring a team of well-respected First Amendment lawyers, he tried to garner more support for freedom of the press in his home state. He started an organization called Ohioans for a Free Press, but soon found that no local newspaper would accept advertisements to publicize the cause and recruit members. He tried another tactic and held a rally. In front of the few hundred people gathered before him, he said: "We're talking about the censorship of a magazine with three million circulation, sold in twenty-five different countries with an estimated fifteen million readers . . . that's fifteen million voices that have a right to be heard . . . now either we have a free press or we don't." [71]

The lack of supporters that night seemed to foreshadow the outcome of the case. The defense lawyers had a considerable challenge ahead of them because they had to prove that *Hustler* was not obscene. Yet, as reporter Bruce Handy describes, the magazine tended to focus on sex that was "bad and ugly and dirty, with women depicted in rape fantasies, smeared with excrement, likened literally to pieces of meat." [72] After a lengthy trial, Flynt's lawyer, Harold Fahringer, eloquently delivered his closing words:

> Freedom doesn't mean anything if it's not offensive. Freedom is putting up with an awful lot in society that is distasteful. Freedom is only meaningful if it includes *all* speech, no matter who is offended by it. . . . The freedom guaran-

teed in the First Amendment is indivisible. You can't take it away from Larry Flynt and keep it for yourself. . . . Watch out, or some day you will find the walls have grown up all around you. [73]

Despite the elegant speech, the jury agreed with prosecutor Leis. For the prosecution's closing argument, he dramatically drew a chalk line across the courtroom floor, saying that Flynt took "the

Flynt is led to jail in handcuffs after being convicted of pandering, obscenity, and engaging in organized crime in 1977.

beautiful thing of sex and reduced it to the level of an animal. . . . It's time to draw the line against obscenity." [74]

Flynt's unconventional behavior in court did not help his cause with the jury and judge. According to one Flynt biography, "The Porn King became as infamous for his outlandish courtroom antics as for his magazine, hurling orange peels and unseemly remarks at judges, and even appearing in court wrapped in a diaper made from the American flag." [75] Siding with the prosecutor, the jury chose to draw a line by entering "guilty" on all counts for Flynt and acquitting his staff members.

A stunned Flynt was handcuffed immediately. When the judge asked if he wanted to speak before he heard his sentence, Flynt found his tongue and angrily responded, "You haven't made an intelligent decision during the course of this trial, and I don't expect one now." [76] The judge slammed his gavel and gave him the maximum sentence: eleven thousand dollars in fines and seven to twenty-five years in prison without bond.

In spite of the long sentence, Flynt ended up serving only six days in jail. His team of lawyers filed an appeal and got him out on bond. Shortly after being released, he and Althea married. He also underwent a religious change of heart under the mentorship of Ruth Carter Stapleton, sister to then-president Jimmy Carter. During this period, he described himself as a born-again Christian, and tried to clean up the content of *Hustler* to offer sexual images that were less demeaning to women and traditional notions of love. Some of his staff members thought he had lost his mind, but they continued to produce *Hustler* under his reformed leadership. It would be years before the appeal to the Cincinnati decision would return to court, and in 1978 he was called to defend another obscenity indictment in Lawrenceville, Georgia. Even though many of his beliefs had changed dramatically, Flynt still believed in absolute freedom of speech. He quickly organized a defense team to fight the indictment.

Never Again the Same

On the first day of the Georgia trial, his life changed forever. While he was walking next to his lawyers outside the courthouse, a hidden sniper fired shots from across the street. Flynt watched his lawyer fall to the ground just as he was shot twice himself. He was rushed to the hospital for emergency treatment that ended up lasting several days. He underwent a series of eleven surgeries, yet the doctors still did not expect him to live. By the time the ordeal was over, he survived but ended up paralyzed from the waist down. Moreover, although he could not move his legs, he still could feel the horrendous pain of his injuries in his torso and legs. He reflects, "I was nearly insane from the constant, excruciating pain. . . . I couldn't think about God anymore, or who might have shot me, or anything else. I was utterly consumed by my agony."[77]

Flynt's personal and professional life turned to shambles. At the time, his condition was incurable. The emotional grief over being paralyzed caused him to lose faith in his newfound Christianity. In addition, the man believed to have shot Flynt was Joseph Paul Franklin, a white supremacist who objected to *Hustler.* Conflicting evidence prevented the police from building a solid case against him. In desperation Flynt searched for anything that would relieve his pain and began abusing prescription and illegal drugs. "I was detoxed three times,"[78] he said of that period. He dropped out of society and neglected his business responsibilities.

Althea took over running *Hustler* and did very well until she, too, turned to drugs to relieve the many pressures in her life. In the midst of their downward spiral, the Cincinnati case was finally heard by the appellate court. The jury's earlier decision to convict Flynt of pandering, obscenity, and organized crime was overturned. Flynt had once again escaped from the legal censorship attempts of his critics, but he was temporarily silenced by an assassin who hated his form of expression.

Jerry Falwell v. Larry Flynt

In 1983 Flynt once again put the obscenity law to the test when he published a fake advertisement for Compari liquor that imitated their ad campaign featuring celebrities who described their first drink. In his parody of the Compari ad, he ran a picture of Moral Majority leader Jerry Falwell describing his "'first time' as a drunken sexual encounter with his mother in an outhouse."[79] Falwell's outrage was not quelled by the disclaimer printed at the bottom of the page: "Ad parody—not to be taken seriously."[80] The televangelist sued the *Hustler* corporation and Flynt for $45 million to amend for invasion of privacy, libel, and intent to inflict emotional distress.

Over a year after running the ad, Flynt was found innocent of libel. According to Richard Lacayo in *Time* magazine, "no reasonable person could think that the spoof was being presented as factual."[81] Falwell and his lawyers appealed the case all the way to the Supreme Court; however, Flynt was ultimately cleared of all charges.

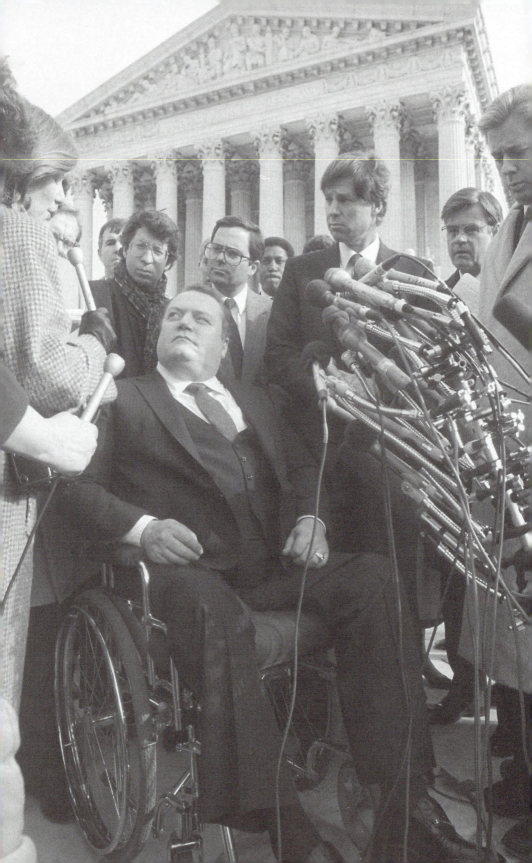

Rodney A. Smolla, who later wrote a book about the *Jerry Falwell v. Larry Flynt* case, characterizes the trial as "a truly remarkable episode in American legal history. . . . The case was as much a cultural battle as a legal battle, a case in which we as a culture put the First Amendment itself on trial." [82]

Victory in the courtroom was sweet for Flynt, but his personal sacrifices for the cause of free speech weighed heavy on his life. He told a reporter for *People* magazine that he would rather have his legs than the courtroom success. Moreover, although corrective surgery to control the excruciating pain from his wounds allowed him to resume full leadership of *Hustler,* he regretted that his wife Althea had become a hopeless drug addict in the process of taking over when he was incapacitated. Shortly after the Supreme Court decision, Althea drowned in her bathtub on June 27, 1987. Flynt believed she had become so weakened from AIDS (likely acquired through intravenous drug use) that she slipped and could not pull herself to safety. Her death was the greatest tragedy of his life.

First Amendment Hero or Depraved Smut Peddler?

In 1996 Flynt published his aptly titled autobiography, *An Unseemly Man: My Life as Pornographer, Pundit, and Social Outcast.* In it he narrates a story about accidentally starting a barn fire when he was three years old. The fire became so hot that it burst the building, sending the roof sailing through the air until it landed on a nearby hill. "In later years I came to think of that event as a metaphor for my life," he writes. "I've unintentionally blown the roof off of social and political institutions, too. I still like to play with fire." [83]

Flynt's explosive effect on American culture inspired a major motion picture in 1996 about his censorship battles titled *The People v. Larry Flynt.* Producer Oliver Stone captures the enigma of Flynt in his commentary about making the movie: "Larry, by some standards, is a First Amendment hero and defender of the Constitution; he is also an exploiter of women and a one-man wrecking crew on 'community standards.' Does he fight the dirty fight for us, or does he only care about a buck, as the head of a sleazy media empire that hides behind a cause? Therein lies the reason Larry Flynt is fascinating." [84]

Whether he is a devil or a saint, or a little of both, Larry Flynt has posed important questions about freedom of speech in the

< *Flynt talks to reporters outside the U.S. Supreme Court in 1987 after the Court decided in his favor in the case of* Jerry Falwell v. Larry Flynt.

twentieth century. He believes that most young people take the First Amendment for granted these days. He writes, "I intend to devote my entire life to the cause of civil liberties and civil rights for all mankind in an effort to bring about peace on earth. I absolutely refuse to compromise my unorthodox strategy concerning my principles, ideas, goals, and conduct that have brought me this far."[85] Larry Flynt's victories in court have set a powerful precedent to protect pornography and political satire under the umbrella of First Amendment freedoms. Even Americans who disagree with his philosophy and tactics cannot deny that he has been one of the most visible fighters against censorship in the United States.

CHAPTER 6

Mitchell Kapor: Free Expression on the Electronic Frontier

For many people, Mitchell (or Mitch) Kapor would fit the definition of a visionary. In the early years of computer technology, he had the foresight and imagination to understand the tremendous potential power available in computer networks to expand human knowledge and communication. Since Kapor's vision of the electronic future has always been rooted in strong democratic values, his innovations and social activism have benefited millions of computer users. Among other major contributions, he has helped to protect the right to free expression in cyberspace for all "netizens." As biographer Steve Schneider notes, "In a time when few understood the rules and bounds of computer networks, he stepped in to insure that people were treated fairly. His role in the shaping of public policy has also limited the scope of government involvement in the creation of information infrastructure and resulted in a less regulated, more free online society." [86] Mitch Kapor is widely recognized as one of the foremost fighters against Internet censorship.

Child of the 1950s, Teen of the 1960s

Mitch was born in Brooklyn, New York, on November 1, 1950, to Jesse and Phoebe Kapor. His paternal grandparents and maternal great-grandparents had been Jewish immigrants from Eastern Europe. Both sides of the family started life in poverty when they resettled in the United States. Their economic struggles improved when Jesse, Mitch's future father, attended the City College of New York and then started a business manufacturing corrugated boxes with Phoebe's brother, a former college classmate. Jesse and Phoebe married and raised Mitch in Brooklyn for three years before they moved to the middle-class neighborhood of Freeport on Long Island. The family company, Corrugated Paper Products Incorporated, remained in Brooklyn.

Since the creation of the Internet, visionary Mitchell Kapor has worked tirelessly to protect freedom of expression in cyberspace.

By the time Mitch reached the second grade he complained of being bored in school, so his parents arranged to advance him into the third grade class. The difficulties he encountered ended up shaping his sensibilities as an adult. As he explains:

> Academically, it was easy to keep up with the work. However, being socially adept was not my strength then, and being a lot younger than all of the other kids made it even harder to fit in. As a consequence, my status as an outsider quickly solidified. I was teased a lot for having buck teeth. . . . I think that my own profound experiences as a social outsider as a child gave me a basis to appreciate other situations of social exclusion and denial of opportunity to others. [87]

The rough school experience did not hinder his enjoyment of many activities as he grew up. An avid Boy Scout, he eventually became a patrol leader and then a Life Scout. His hero, Willie Mays, inspired him to play Little League baseball for several years. From the age of ten until his bar mitzvah at the age of thirteen, he went to Hebrew school three days a week. He also took clarinet lessons and played in the junior high school band. During summers, camping was a favorite family event that taught him "to love hiking, swimming, and roasting marshmallows and listening to ghost stories around the campfire." [88]

Kapor characterizes himself as a "math nerd" during his school years. His academic talent earned him the rank of captain of the math team in high school, and he graduated when he was only sixteen years old. He also spent Saturdays at Columbia University's high school science honors program where he was introduced to programming computers in 1965 and 1966. "I was very interested," says Kapor, "and then I went off to college and got distracted by drugs, sex and rock and roll, like anybody with half a brain would have then!" [89]

Kapor participated in the youth counterculture of the 1960s during and after college. He experimented with LSD and "always was searching for some sort of 'enlightenment.'" [90] However, the social experimentation did not distract him from earning a bachelor's degree at Yale University in 1971. He studied psychology, linguistics,

Students demonstrate at Yale University in 1970. While a student at Yale in the late 1960s and early 1970s, Kapor engaged in the widespread social experimentation of the time.

and computer science as part of a unique major in cybernetics. Although he enjoyed his college classes in computer science, it would be several years before he rediscovered his intense interest in computers. "I spent my best time at Yale," he says, "at the college radio station as music director and program director, playing free-form rock and roll on the air." [91]

Looking for a Purpose in Life

As a young man, Kapor dabbled in many different occupations. After college he became a rock disc jockey in Hartford, Connecticut, and then tried to make a living as a stand-up comic. In 1973 he moved to Boston to start a job programming mainframe computers, but he ended up hating the work. "Programming in those days was much more about keeping track of a lot of arbitrary details," he says. "I was attracted to the more intimate 1:1 nature of personal computers and of the idea that they should be tools to serve human needs for information and communication." [92]

At age twenty-five he found himself unemployed and at the end of a troublesome four-year marriage. Again, the promise of spiritual enlightenment lured him to a Switzerland retreat to study transcendental meditation, a deep relaxation technique that can enhance mental awareness, creativity, health, and spirituality. The program promised to teach the ability to levitate through a rigorous practice that included as much as fourteen hours of meditation a day. Kapor became disillusioned when the promise of levitation never materialized, so he returned to the United States to complete a graduate degree in counseling psychology in 1978. After graduating, he tried his hand at becoming a counselor for the New England Memorial Hospital in Stoneham, Massachusetts. He discovered that the career did not appeal to him, calling it "the psychic equivalent of emptying bedpans." [93] Kapor says of this aimless time in his life, "My rep[utation] was [that I was] a very bright kid with a lot of potential who hasn't found himself. Almost thirty. Sort of lost." [94]

His drifting soon ended, largely due to an unexpected opportunity. Unemployment gave him extra time to explore the new personal computer equipment on the market. He quickly became hooked. Low on funds, the only way he could purchase his first Apple II was to sell his stereo. While he was in the computer store, he overheard a man ask a clerk for help in purchasing a new computer. Kapor knew enough to offer his advice. His confidence and knowledge convinced the man to hire Kapor to become his teacher for five dollars an hour. Soon Kapor was hiring himself out on a regular basis as an

Kapor founded the Lotus Development Corporation with partner Jonathan Sachs in 1982. Their Lotus 1-2-3 spreadsheet program produced profits greater than any other software program in history.

independent computer consultant. He taught himself more advanced computer applications and developed software programs on his own. Kapor had found his true vocation. "It was a total cottage industry by a marginal consultant," he says. "That's how I got started, honest to God." [95]

Recognizing his talent, a friend encouraged him to go to Massachusetts Institute of Technology (MIT) for a master's in business administration. He began the program at MIT, but stayed only seven months because Apple computers offered him a job to work for VisiCalc, their business program in Silicon Valley, California. In his characteristic style, he became bored with California in six months and returned to Boston. Meanwhile, a spreadsheet program called VisiPlot that he and a friend had developed for VisiCalc became an instant success. He sold the program for $12 million and used the money to open his own business.

Building a Software Empire

In 1982 Kapor joined with partner Jonathan Sachs to found the Lotus Development Corporation, a company name that was inspired by Kapor's early interest in Eastern mysticism. Within a year Kapor developed their most lucrative application, the famous spreadsheet program called Lotus 1-2-3. As reporter Bruce Sterling writes, the invention was "one of the most spectacularly successful business ventures of the later twentieth century." [96] The innovative software offered the usual spreadsheet features but was much quicker and provided the first on-screen help and tutorial program. The assistance of a customer support department, which was unheard of at the time, was also part of the package. Profits soared above any other software program in history. By its third year, Lotus was making $258 million a year in revenue. Lotus 1-2-3 is still one of the most widely used software programs in the world.

Yet, Mitch Kapor was never one to feel comfortable in the big corporate world. As his company grew into a bureaucratic empire, he lost his enthusiasm for coming to work each day. Selling his portion of Lotus Development Corporation for $40 million, Kapor left to be on his own once again. After he resigned, he founded and directed ON Technology from 1987 to 1990 and taught media arts and sciences on the side at MIT. If Kapor had stayed with Lotus, it is likely that he would be as wealthy as Bill Gates of Microsoft, who is a multibillionaire and the richest man in the world. Money, however, was never the only interest in Kapor's life. Another of his computer-related passions would soon inspire him to become one of the most influential fighters against censorship in the late twentieth century.

A Visit from the FBI

The passion that quickly developed in the early 1990s was Kapor's vision for the future of the Internet. Long before others did, he anticipated the development of the World Wide Web, an information superhighway connecting millions of computer users in America and the world. An incident in 1990 made him realize how important it would be to ensure that civil liberties were protected in the electronic frontier, just as they were in the United States. Kapor was visited by local Federal Bureau of Investigation (FBI) agents in his office and then carted off like a criminal to be fingerprinted at the FBI offices. The reason for this FBI fiasco was that he had inadvertently received a file that some teenage hackers had spread around the Internet after breaking into the computer records of the AT&T corporation. His treatment was unjustified because he had not violated any law.

Through this experience, Kapor found out that the U.S. Secret Service was conducting what they called "Operation Sun Devil," a two-year investigation which involved 150 federal agents, several local and state law enforcement agencies, and the combined security forces of corporations like PacBell, AT&T, MCI, and American Express. The purpose of the investigation was to root out anonymous computer hackers who were allegedly breaking into corporate and government computer files. Yet the FBI and the Secret Service knew little about the inner workings of the Internet at that time. Their ignorance led to mistakes that Kapor believed compromised the rights of ordinary American citizens.

Meeting John Perry Barlow

Kapor might not have given the incident any more attention than his passing irritation if it were not for a message he saw posted on one of his favorite computer bulletin boards, the Whole Earth 'Lectronic Link, known by its regular visitors as the WELL. John Perry Barlow wrote an account of how he also had been visited by a federal law officer in his Pinedale, Wyoming, home. He described his two-hour interview by Special Agent Richard Baxter Jr. Barlow was best known as the lyricist for the Grateful Dead band since 1970. He was also a member of a third-generation cattle-ranching family and a Wyoming native, but in the late 1980s he had sold the ranch to become a computer telecommunications devotee. He described himself as a "techno-crank." [97]

Barlow had done some homework on the FBI operation and learned that the agents involved had ransacked several family homes, shut down several computer bulletin boards, confiscated over forty computers, seized twenty-three thousand disks, lost about 5.4 million pages of information, and generally trampled on the First and Fourth Amendments to the U.S. Constitution. Barlow himself was not arrested or even accused of any crime, but he was questioned about his association with some underground hackers. He was outraged that innocent computer enthusiasts, who had done nothing illegal, were being watched and bullied by the federal government.

Barlow writes,

> I decided it was time to speak up. The evening of my visit from Agent Baxter, I wrote an account of it which I placed on the WELL. Several days later, Mitch Kapor literally dropped by for a chat. . . . We talked for a couple of hours in my office while a spring snowstorm swirled outside. When I recounted for him what I had learned about Operation Sun Devil, he decided it was time for him to speak up too. [98]

For Kapor, Barlow's post had clarified the danger of the FBI's dragnet. He flew in his private jet to meet with Barlow in Pinedale. Together they started the Electronic Frontier Foundation (EFF).

The Electronic Frontier Foundation

Very soon after that meeting, Barlow wrote a manifesto titled "Crime and Puzzlement" and distributed it on the WELL. The document stated that he and Kapor were founding the EFF to ensure that constitutional rights and protections were respected in cyberspace. They worked to preserve the positive definition of a computer "hacker" as someone who openly shared programs and information in order to make the Internet accessible to more people. The digital highway had the potential to preserve some of the best qualities of a true democracy, and Kapor and Barlow wanted to educate users to promote freedom of speech and ethical communication.

As one reporter observed, "The sudden declaration of a coherent, politicized counter-strike from the ranks of hackerdom electrified the community." [99] Kapor and Barlow formally announced the formation of the EFF in Washington on July 10. They started off by helping to pay for lawyers for those wrongly accused as dangerous hackers, and began to work toward ensuring that the Bill of Rights would apply to digital media. "Free expression must be preserved long after the last printing press is gathering museum dust," Barlow explained in another manifesto sent to supporters. "And we intend an unequivocal legal demonstration that speech is speech whether it finds form in ink or in ascii." [100]

Within the first year, the new nonprofit organization funded a two-year project focusing on computers and civil liberties to teach policy makers and law enforcement agencies about civil rights in cyberspace and telecommunications policy. Kapor and Barlow also met with congressional staffers, legal authorities, journalists, White House officials, and the Library of Congress to lobby for freedom of speech on the Internet. There was tremendous support from the onset as word got out about the organization. Barlow alone received between fifty and one hundred e-mail messages a day and Kapor found that many people were interested in donating funds to develop the EFF (Kapor himself had provided the initial funding). Kapor became the president of the organization and the press coverage immediately became intense. Civil liberties on the information superhighway was a hot topic.

Soon the EFF had its own Internet node where people could log on to the "eff.org." They published print and online journals and maintained a huge archive of information about anticensorship,

John Perry Barlow, in concert with Kapor, founded the Electronic Frontier Foundation (EFF) in the late 1980s to ensure the protection of civil liberties in cyberspace.

electronic civil rights, privacy issues, and academic freedom. The national headquarters in Cambridge, Massachusetts, began to employ a full-time staff. More than thirty civil rights lawyers offered to do pro bono work in defense of the Constitution in cyberspace.

In addition to launching extensive education campaigns, the EFF filed a suit against several U.S. Secret Service agents to address violations of the First and Fourth Amendments during Operation Sun Devil. Kapor explained the reason for the legal action in *Scientific American* magazine in 1991:

> The EFF is not seeking confrontation for its own sake. One of the realities of our legal system is that one often has to fight for a legal or constitutional right in the courts in order to get it recognized outside the courts. One goal of

the lawsuit is to establish clear grounds under which search and seizure of electronic media is "unreasonable" and unjust. Another is to establish the clear applicability of First Amendment principles to the new media. [101]

The problem, according to Kapor, is that any users could be targeted and censored for their computer activities. "The hackers were the first in the line of fire," says Kapor, "but now civilians are getting it too. If a bulletin board is seized because of one hacker's actions, what about the rights of other users?" [102] In the 1990s bulletin boards were some of the main Internet sites where people online could share opinions and information. As Internet reporter Esther Dyson wrote about the legal action, "The First Amendment protects my right to peaceably assemble in protest of government policies. Well, a bulletin board is the way a computer-literate society assembles for a redress of grievances." [103]

Fighting Against Internet Censorship

The EFF's influence grew rapidly and the organizational offices were moved to Washington, D.C., to be closer to national politics and government. As Kapor had anticipated, the World Wide Web was becoming a reality; more and more average Americans were obtaining personal computers and logging on to the Internet. Under President Bill Clinton's administration, expansion of the "data highway" became a pet project of Vice President Al Gore. Gore credited Kapor for much of the drafting of the plans for the National Information Infrastructure. In the 1990s Kapor quickly became a star witness at congressional hearings and gained easy access to the White House. The federal government was finally "in sync" with the philosophy of the EFF.

Today the EFF maintains a huge website that features up-to-the-minute information about legal cases related to Internet freedom of expression. The site's Blue Ribbon Campaign to fight Internet censorship provides law and policy information, media resources, and an action center describing how to fight for Internet civil liberties. The extensive archive collects alerts about incidents of censorship across the globe.

Kapor often compares his vision of the EFF to the democratic ideal of Thomas Jefferson. He wants to make the Internet accessible

< *Vice President Al Gore, a champion for expanding access to the Internet, acknowledged Kapor for his contributions in the creation of the National Information Infrastructure.*

so more people can use it. Although he cherishes the atmosphere of freedom in cyberspace, he believes that absolute freedom is dangerous and ultimately reduces the participation of ordinary citizens. The electronic frontier must be civilized by the average user, not the elite technophile. As he said in a 1993 interview, "The Internet is an open system, everything is published, everything gets argued about, basically by anybody who can get in. Mostly, it's exclusive and elitist just because it's so difficult. Let's make it easier to use." [104] Open access will bring more users into the network, which in turn will lubricate entrepreneurship in order to give people more market choice.

More importantly, he says, the participation of the citizenry will "guarantee free cultural and political expression—the extension of the First Amendment into cyberspace." [105] According to Kapor's philosophy, the best way to help the Internet bring humanity together is to preserve individual liberty, promote diversity, and develop a sense of cyberspace community.

Electronic Exploration and Cyber Citizenship

These days, Kapor continues to work for the principles he believes will ensure a viable democratic future for electronic communication. As trustee of the Level Playing Field Institute, he helps to enhance equal opportunity in the workplace and to support the values of an inclusive society. In projects affiliated with the University of California, he promotes educational diversity programs for underserved students interested in math and science. Moreover, the Mitchell Kapor Foundation that he endowed conducts research into the social impact of information technology and the intersection of health and the environment. His encouragement and financial support have inspired many "netizens" to pioneer new programs and companies on the electronic frontier. Somewhere in between all these activities, he finds time to enjoy life with his wife, two teenage children, and two dogs in their San Francisco home.

Internet reporter Bruce Sterling pays tribute to Kapor in his book *The Hacker Crackdown: Law and Disorder on the Electronic Frontier:*

> There were many stellar figures in the civil libertarian community. There's no question, however, that its single most influential figure was Mitchell D. Kapor. Other people might have formal titles, or governmental positions, have more experience with crime, or with the law, or with the arcanities of computer security or constitutional theory. But by 1991 Kapor

had transcended any such narrow role. . . . Mitch had become the central civil-libertarian ad-hocrat. Mitch had stood up first, he had spoken out loudly, directly, vigorously and angrily, he had put his own reputation, and his very considerable personal fortune, on the line. By mid-'91 Kapor was the best-known advocate of his cause and was known PERSONALLY by almost every single human being in America with any direct influence on the question of civil liberties in cyberspace.[106]

Although Kapor has made many remarkable contributions to the world of computer technology, he certainly will be remembered as a leading fighter against censorship in cyberspace.

NOTES

Chapter 1: James Madison: Founder of American Free Speech

1. Quoted in Merrill D. Peterson, ed., *James Madison: A Biography in His Own Words.* New York: Newsweek, 1974, p. 20.

2. Quoted in Richard L. Blanco and Paul J. Sanborn, eds., *The American Revolution: An Encyclopedia.* Vol. 2. New York: Garland, 1993, p. 1002.

3. Jack N. Rakove, *James Madison and the Creation of the American Republic.* New York: Longman, 2002, p. 4.

4. Quoted in Rakove, *James Madison and the Creation of the American Republic,* p. 6.

5. Quoted in Peterson, *James Madison,* p. 30.

6. Quoted in Rob Boston, "James Madison and Church-State Separation," *Church & State,* March 2001, p. 12.

7. Quoted in Rakove, *James Madison and the Creation of the American Republic,* p. 12.

8. Boston, "James Madison and Church-State Separation," p. 11.

9. Carl T. Bogus, "Jefferson's Patsy?" *Nation,* July 8, 2002, p. 30.

10. Quoted in Robert J. Morgan, *James Madison on the Constitution and the Bill of Rights.* New York: Greenwood, 1988, p. 163.

11. Rakove, *James Madison and the Creation of the American Republic,* p. 98.

12. Quoted in InfoUSA, "The Bill of Rights," 2003. www.usinfo. state.gov.

13. The White House, "Dolley Payne Todd Madison," 2003. www. whitehouse.gov.

14. Quoted in Peterson, *James Madison,* p. 407.

15. Sheila Suess Kennedy, *Free Expression in America: A Documentary History.* Westport, CT: Greenwood, 1999, p. 29.

Chapter 2: Theodore Schroeder: Testing the First Amendment

16. Quoted in Jeffery A. Smith, *War and Press Freedom: The Problem of Prerogative Power.* New York: Oxford University Press, 1999, p. 43.

17. Quoted in Southern Illinois University at Carbondale Library, "Theodore Schroeder Papers: Biography," 2003. www.lib. siu.edu.

18. Quoted in David M. Rabban, *Free Speech in Its Forgotten Years.* Cambridge: Cambridge University Press, 1997, p. 50.

19. Quoted in Rabban, *Free Speech in Its Forgotten Years,* p. 51.

20. Quoted in Ann K. Symons and Sally Gardner Reed, eds., *Speaking Out! Voices in Celebration of Intellectual Freedom.* Chicago: American Library Association, 1999, p. 54.

21. Quoted in Rabban, *Free Speech in Its Forgotten Years,* p. 60.

22. Quoted in Rabban, *Free Speech in Its Forgotten Years,* p. 53.

23. Rabban, *Free Speech in Its Forgotten Years,* p. 49.

24. Quoted in Rabban, *Free Speech in Its Forgotten Years,* p. 63.

25. Quoted in Rabban, *Free Speech in Its Forgotten Years,* p. 63.

26. Theodore Schroeder, ed., *Free Press Anthology.* New York: Free Speech League, 1909, p. i.

27. Theodore Schroeder, *"Obscene" Literature and Constitutional Law.* New York: Privately printed, 1911, p. 98.

28. Theodore Schroeder, *Constitutional Free Speech Defined and Defended: An Unfinished Argument in a Case of Blasphemy.* New York: Free Speech League, 1919, pp. 20–21.

29. Quoted in Rabban, *Free Speech in Its Forgotten Years,* p. 53.

30. Quoted in Rabban, *Free Speech in Its Forgotten Years,* p. 75.

31. Quoted in Rabban, *Free Speech in Its Forgotten Years,* p. 54.

Chapter 3: Emma Goldman: Anticensorship Freedom Fighter

32. Quoted in Martha Solomon, *Emma Goldman.* Boston: Twayne, 1987, p. 8.

33. Quoted in Alix Kates Shulman, *Red Emma Speaks: An Emma Goldman Reader.* Atlantic Highlands, NJ: Humanities Press, 1996, p. 140.

34. Quoted in Emma Goldman, *Living My Life.* Mineola, NY: Dover, 1930, p. 12.

35. Quoted in Berkeley Digital Library SunSITE, "Life and Conflict in the New World," *Emma Goldman Papers,* 2003. http://sunsite. berkeley.edu.

36. Shulman, *Red Emma Speaks,* p. 22.

37. Quoted in Shulman, *Red Emma Speaks,* p. 22.

38. Quoted in Peter Glassgold, ed., *Anarchy! An Anthology of Emma Goldman's* Mother Earth. Washington, DC: Counterpoint, 2001, p. 5.

39. Goldman, *Living My Life,* p. 51.

40. Glassgold, *Anarchy!* p. xv.

41. Quoted in Shulman, *Red Emma Speaks,* p. 56.

42. Quoted in *Scholastic Update,* "Red Emma," December 8, 1995, p. 17.

43. Quoted in Berkeley Digital Library SunSITE, "Introduction," *Emma Goldman Papers,* 2003. http://sunsite.berkeley.edu.

44. Quoted in Glassgold, *Anarchy!* p. xxxiii.

45. Quoted in Shulman, *Red Emma Speaks,* p. 437.

46. Berkeley Digital Library SunSITE, "Introduction," *Emma Goldman Papers.*

Chapter 4: Tommy Smothers: Comedy Against Censorship

47. Mike Duffy, "'Smothered' Revisits Brothers' Battle with CBS," *Detroit Free Press,* December 3, 2002.

48. Marsala Rypka, "Up Close and Personal," *Las Vegas Magazine,* Smobro Press Room, 2003. www.smothersbrothers.com.

49. Quoted in Rypka, "Up Close and Personal."

50. Quoted in Aniko Bodroghkozy, *Groove Tube: Sixties Television and the Youth Rebellion.* Durham, NC: Duke University Press, 2001, p. 125.

51. Quoted in *Smothered: The Censorship Struggles of the Smothers Brothers Comedy Hour,* prod. and dir. Maureen Muldaur, New Video Group, 2003.

52. Quoted in *Smothered.*

53. Michael Kilian, "Documentary Recounts Struggle for Free Speech on the Tube," *Chicago Tribune,* November 11, 2002.

54. Quoted in *Smothered.*

55. Quoted in *Smothered.*

56. Quoted in *Smothered.*

57. Bodroghkozy, *Groove Tube,* p. 130.

58. Quoted in Bodroghkozy, *Groove Tube,* p. 131.

59. Quoted in *Smothered*.

60. Quoted in *Smothered*.

61. Quoted in *Smothered*.

62. Quoted in *Smothered*.

63. Quoted in The Smothers Brothers, "Remick Ridge Vineyards," 2003. www.smothersbrothers.com.

64. Quoted in Rypka, "Up Close and Personal."

Chapter 5: Larry Flynt: "I Absolutely Refuse to Compromise"

65. Quoted in Infotrac, "Larry Flynt," Biography Resource Center, February 2000. http://infotrac.galenet.

66. Larry Flynt, *An Unseemly Man: My Life as Pornographer, Pundit, and Social Outcast.* Los Angeles: Newstar, 1996, p. 8.

67. Flynt, *An Unseemly Man*, p. 14.

68. Flynt, *An Unseemly Man*, p. 39.

69. Quoted in Infotrac, "Larry Flynt."

70. Flynt, *An Unseemly Man*, p. 81.

71. Flynt, *An Unseemly Man*, p. 126.

72. Quoted in Infotrac, "Larry Flynt."

73. Flynt, *An Unseemly Man*, p. 151.

74. Flynt, *An Unseemly Man*, p. 152.

75. Quoted in Infotrac, "Larry Flynt."

76. Flynt, *An Unseemly Man*, p. 155.

77. Flynt, *An Unseemly Man*, p. 177.

78. Quoted in Infotrac, "Larry Flynt."

79. Sean R. Pollock, ed., "Larry Flynt," *Newsmakers 1997 Cumulation: The People Behind the News.* Farmington Hills, MI: Gale Group, May 1997.

80. Pollock, "Larry Flynt."

81. Quoted in Pollock, "Larry Flynt."

82. Rodney A. Smolla, *Jerry Falwell v. Larry Flynt: The First Amendment on Trial.* New York: St. Martin's, 1988, preface.

83. Flynt, *An Unseemly Man*, p. 10.

84. Flynt, *An Unseemly Man*, pp. xi–xii.

85. Quoted in Infotrac, "Larry Claxton Flynt," *The Complete Marquis Who's Who*, Biography Resource Center, 2001. http://infotrac.galenet.com.

Chapter 6: Mitchell Kapor: Free Expression on the Electronic Frontier

86. Steve Schneider, "Mitch Kapor," February 16, 1997. http://ei.cs.vt.edu/~history/Kapor.Schneider.html.

87. Mitchell Kapor, e-mail interview by author, September 1, 2003.

88. Kapor, e-mail interview.

89. Quoted in Bruce Sterling, *The Hacker Crackdown: Law and Disorder on the Electronic Frontier*. New York: Bantam, 1993, p. 191.

90. Quoted in Schneider, "Mitch Kapor."

91. Kapor, e-mail interview.

92. Kapor, e-mail interview.

93. Quoted in Robert Wright, "Mitch Kapor, Data Highway Guru," *GNN Magazine*, October 4, 1993. www.cd.sc.ehu.es/DOCS/nearnet.gnn.com/mag/10_93/articles/kapor/nkapor.intro.html.

94. Quoted in Sterling, *The Hacker Crackdown*, p. 192.

95. Sterling, *The Hacker Crackdown*, p. 192.

96. Sterling, *The Hacker Crackdown*, p. 193.

97. Sterling, *The Hacker Crackdown*, p. 155.

98. John Perry Barlow, "Crime and Puzzlement," Electronic Frontier Foundation, June 8, 1990. www.eff.org.

99. Sterling, *The Hacker Crackdown*, p. 163.

100. John Perry Barlow, "Crime and Puzzlement 2," Electronic Frontier Foundation, July 21, 1990. www.eff.org.

101. Mitchell Kapor, "Civil Liberties in Cyberspace," *Scientific American*, September 1991. www.eff.org.

102. Quoted in Esther Dyson, "Hacker's Rights," *Forbes*, January 7, 1991, p. 288.

103. Dyson, "Hacker's Rights," p. 288.

104. Quoted in Sterling, *The Hacker Crackdown*, p. 194.

105. Quoted in Wright, "Mitch Kapor, Data Highway Guru."

106. Sterling, *The Hacker Crackdown*, p. 188.

FOR FURTHER READING

Books

John Chalberg, *Emma Goldman: American Individualist.* Boston: Addison-Wesley, 1997. A good starting point for those interested in Goldman's life and anarchism. This accessible biography includes bibliographic references for further research.

Jean Fritz, *The Great Little Madison.* New York: Putnam, 1989. An engaging biography written especially for young adult readers. It includes details about Madison's personal life along with historical information.

Benton F. Gup and Herbert N. Foerstel, *Banned in the Media: A Reference Guide to Censorship in the Press, Motion Pictures, Broadcasting, and the Internet.* Westport, CT: Greenwood, 1998. A history of media censorship from colonial times to the present in the United States with a bibliography and list of organizations.

Maureen Harrison and Steve Gilbert, *Obscenity and Pornography Decisions of the United States Supreme Court.* West Yorkshire, England: Excellent Books, 2000. Fifteen major court decisions described in easy-to-understand language.

Marvin Meyers, *The Mind of the Founder: Sources of the Political Thought of James Madison.* Lebanon, NH: University Press of New England, 1981. A selection of writings by James Madison with a bibliography.

Eric D. Nuzum, *Parental Advisory: Music Censorship in America.* New York: Quill, 2001. History of music censorship focused on the 1950s to 2001, but includes incidents dating back to the nineteenth century. Includes an extensive chronology and a bibliography.

Pete Seeger, *The Incompleat Folksinger.* Lincoln: University of Nebraska Press, 1992. A collection of essays by Pete Seeger with photos and music notation.

Internet Sources

The Museum of Broadcast Communications, "The Smothers Brothers Comedy Hour," 2003. www.museum.tv.

Websites

The Emma Goldman Papers (http://sunsite.berkeley.edu). This website provides an extensive collection of historical and biographical information about Emma Goldman, including electronic text of original documents.

The James Madison Center (www.jmu.edu). A repository of information about Madison and the Revolutionary and Early Republican eras of American History.

Larry Flynt.com (www.larryflynt.com). Larry Flynt maintains this website to report on *Hustler* magazine's position on issues such as free speech, individual rights, and civil liberties.

Mitchell Kapor Home Page (www.kei.com). Provides a biography, articles by Kapor, and his web log.

Pete Seeger Appreciation Page (http://home.earthlink.net). This website includes recordings of Pete Seeger songs, a biography, a discography, and a photo gallery.

The Smothers Brothers (www.smothersbrothers.com). Official website of the Smothers Brothers that includes biographies, recordings, performance history, and current information about Tom and Dick Smothers.

WORKS CONSULTED

Books

Richard L. Blanco and Paul J. Sanborn, eds., *The American Revolution: An Encyclopedia*. Vol. 2. New York: Garland, 1993. Seven hundred historical sketches and four hundred biographical sketches related to the Revolutionary War, with illustrations.

Aniko Bodroghkozy, *Groove Tube: Sixties Television and the Youth Rebellion*. Durham, NC: Duke University Press, 2001. An examination of the cultural impact of television during the 1960s in the United States.

Candace Falk, *Love, Anarchy, and Emma Goldman*. New Brunswick, NJ: Rutgers University Press, 1990. A biography of Emma Goldman emphasizing her personal relationships and their impact on her work.

Larry Flynt, *An Unseemly Man: My Life as Pornographer, Pundit, and Social Outcast*. Los Angeles: Newstar, 1996. An explicit autobiography covering Larry Flynt's life from birth until the 1990s.

Peter Glassgold, ed., *Anarchy! An Anthology of Emma Goldman's Mother Earth*. Washington, DC: Counterpoint, 2001. The collected essays published in *Mother Earth* magazine.

Emma Goldman, *Living My Life*. Mineola, NY: Dover, 1930. Goldman's autobiography describes her personal, philosophical, and political journey through her life.

Sheila Suess Kennedy, *Free Expression in America: A Documentary History*. Westport, CT: Greenwood, 1999. A collection of more than one hundred primary documents about free speech and censorship from 1215 to 1998.

Ralph Ketcham, *James Madison*. Charlottesville, VA: University Press of Virginia, 1991. A thorough overview of Madison's life from birth to death.

Robert J. Morgan, *James Madison on the Constitution and the Bill of Rights*. New York: Greenwood, 1988. Examination of Madison's perspective on the Constitution and Bill of Rights.

Merrill D. Peterson, ed., *James Madison: A Biography in His Own Words*. New York: Newsweek, 1974. A collection of Madison's writings with historical and biographical commentary.

Sean R. Pollock, ed., *Newsmakers 1997 Cumulation: The People Behind the News*. Farmington Hills, MI: Gale Group, May 1997. A reference book with entries about key people who made headlines during the year. Includes a biographical overview of Larry Flynt.

David M. Rabban, *Free Speech in Its Forgotten Years*. Cambridge. Cambridge University Press, 1997. A history of American controversies and court cases about free speech from the Civil War to World War I.

Jack N. Rakove, *James Madison and the Creation of the American Republic*. New York: Longman, 2002. An in-depth biography that offers insight into Madison's political philosophy.

Robert Santelli, Holly George-Warren, and Jim Brown, eds., *American Roots Music*. New York: Harry N. Abrams, 2001. A documentary history of folk music with copious photographs and illustrations.

Theodore Schroeder, ed., *Constitutional Free Speech Defined and Defended: An Unfinished Argument in a Case of Blasphemy*. New York: Free Speech League, 1919. An examination of free speech in court cases before 1919.

———, *Free Press Anthology*. New York: Free Speech League, 1909. A collection of essays about freedom of the press by authors from John Milton to Theodore Schroeder.

———, *"Obscene" Literature and Constitutional Law*. New York: privately printed, 1911. A legal defense of freedom of the press in relation to the definitions of obscenity.

Alix Kates Shulman, *Red Emma Speaks: An Emma Goldman Reader*. Atlantic Highlands, NJ: Humanities Press, 1996. A collection of Emma Goldman's writings and speeches with a concise biographical introduction.

Jeffery A. Smith, *War and Press Freedom: The Problem of Prerogative Power*. New York: Oxford University Press, 1999. A historical examination of the tension between freedom of the press and censorship to preserve national security during times of war.

Rodney A. Smolla, *Jerry Falwell v. Larry Flynt: The First Amendment on Trial*. New York: St. Martin's, 1988. A detailed legal and cultural account of the *Falwell v. Flynt* court case over issues of obscenity and libel.

Martha Solomon, *Emma Goldman*. Boston: Twayne, 1987. A biography of Emma Goldman emphasizing her role as a writer and speaker.

Bruce Sterling, *The Hacker Crackdown: Law and Disorder on the Electronic Frontier*. New York: Bantam, 1993. An examination of the 1990 assault on hackers, when law enforcement officials arrested scores of suspected illicit hackers and other computer-based law breakers.

Ann K. Symons and Sally Gardner Reed, eds., *Speaking Out! Voices in Celebration of Intellectual Freedom*. Chicago: American Library Association, 1999. A collection of quotes and essays defending intellectual freedom.

Periodicals

Carl T. Bogus, "Jefferson's Patsy?" *Nation*, July 8, 2002.

Rob Boston, "James Madison and Church-State Separation," *Church & State*, March 2001.

Tom Chaffin, "Keeping the Faith," *Horizon*, October 1981.

Richard Corliss, "Seeing Red," *Time*, April 9, 1984.

Mike Duffy, "'Smothered' Revisits Brothers' Battle with CBS," *Detroit Free Press*, December 3, 2002.

Esther Dyson, "Hacker's Rights," *Forbes*, January 7, 1991.

Mitchell Kapor, "Kapor on Cyberdharma," *Feed*, June 5, 1998.

———, "Where Is the Digital Highway Really Heading? The Case for a Jeffersonian Information Policy," *Wired*, July/August, 1993.

Michael Kilian, "Documentary Recounts Struggle for Free Speech on the Tube," *Chicago Tribune*, November 11, 2002.

Scholastic Update, "Red Emma," December 8, 1995.

Laura Smith, "Way Too Hot to Handle," *Entertainment Weekly*, March 31, 1995.

Leslie Ware, "Pete Seeger: Keeping the Dream," *Sierra*, March/April 1989.

Internet Sources

John Perry Barlow, "Crime and Puzzlement," Electronic Frontier Foundation, June 8, 1990. www.eff.org.

———, "Crime and Puzzlement 2," Electronic Frontier Foundation, July 21, 1990. www.eff.org.

Berkeley Digital Library SunSITE, "Emma Goldman and Free Speech," *Emma Goldman Papers*, 2003. http://sunsite.berkeley.edu.

———, "Introduction," *Emma Goldman Papers*, 2003. http://sunsite.berkeley.edu.

———, "Life and Conflict in the New World," *Emma Goldman Papers*, 2003. http://sunsite.berkeley.edu.

Cornell Law School, "Bill of Rights," June 6, 2003. www.law.cornell.edu.

Infotrac, "Larry Claxton Flynt," *The Complete Marquis Who's Who*, Biography Resource Center, 2001. http://infotrac.galenet.com.

————, "Larry Flynt," Biography Resource Center, February 2000. http://infotrac.galenet.com.

InfoUSA, "The Bill of Rights," 2003. www.usinfo.state.gov.

————, "The Constitution of the United States," 2003. www.usinfo.state.gov/usa/infousa/facts/funddocs/consteng.htm.

————, "Virginia Statute for Religious Freedom," 2003. www.usinfo.state.gov/usa/infousa/facts/democrac/42.htm.

Mitchell Kapor, "Civil Liberties in Cyberspace," *Scientific American,* September 1991. www.eff.org.

Marsala Rypka, "Up Close and Personal," *Las Vegas Magazine,* Smobro Press Room, 2003. www.smothersbrothers.com.

Steve Schneider, "Mitch Kapor," February 16, 1997. http://ei.cs.vt.edu/~history/Kapor.Schneider.html.

The Smothers Brothers, "Remick Ridge Vineyards," 2003. www.smothersbrothers.com

Southern Illinois University at Carbondale Library, "Theodore Schroeder Papers: Biography," 2003. www.lib.siu.edu.

Spartacus Educational, "Pete Seeger," August 16, 2002. www.spartacus.schoolnet.co.uk.

The White House, "Dolley Payne Todd Madison," 2003. www.whitehouse.gov.

Robert Wright, "Mitch Kapor, Data Highway Guru," *GNN Magazine,* October 4, 1993. http://www.cd.sc.ehu.es/DOCS/nearnet.gnn.com/mag/10_93/articles/kapor/nkapor. intro.html.

Videos

Smothered: The Censorship Struggles of the Smothers Brothers Comedy Hour, prod. and dir. Maureen Muldaur, New Video Group, 2003. A documentary with interviews and footage from the original television show.

INDEX

television, 52, 56–58, 59–62
Todd, Dolley Payne. *See*
   Madison, Dolley
Unseemly Man: My Life as
   Pornographer, Pundit, and
   Social Outcast, An (Larry
   Flynt), 77

"What I Believe" (Goldman),
   48
Whole Earth 'Lectronic Link
   (WELL), 85–86
Williams, Mason, 56
World Wide Web, 84–91

PICTURE CREDITS

Cover Images: Blackbirch Press, Deidre Davidson/SAGA/Landov, Fred Prouser/Reuters/Landov, © Time Life Pictures/Getty Images

AP/Wide World Photos, 63, 66, 70, 73, 76, 88

© Bettmann/CORBIS, 19, 31, 32, 40, 47, 54, 81

CBS/Landov, 58, 61

© Jacques M. Chenet/CORBIS, 10

© CORBIS, 49

© CORBIS SYGMA, 69

© Henry Diltz/CORBIS, 57

© Getty Images, 9

© Hulton/Archive by Getty Images, 27, 28, 44, 53

Kapor Enterprises, Inc., 80

© Ed Kashi/CORBIS, 87

Landov, 14

© Picture History, 16, 20, 23, 36, 43

© Ed Quinn/CORBIS, 83

ABOUT THE AUTHOR

Kate Burns lives in Denver, Colorado, with her partner, Sheila, and their cat and iguana. She received her bachelor of arts degree from Colorado State University and her master of arts degree from the University of California, San Diego. She currently works as a free-lance writer and editor, and teaches writing at community colleges and universities near her home.